The Little Prince

By the author of

NIGHT FLIGHT

WIND, SAND AND STARS

SOUTHERN MAIL

FLIGHT TO ARRAS

AIRMAN'S ODYSSEY

LETTER TO A HOSTAGE

WISDOM OF THE SANDS

"I believe that for his escape he took advantage of the migration of a flock of wild birds."

The Little Prince

Written and Illustrated by

Antoine de Saint Exupéry

Translated from the French
by Katherine Woods

A Harvest/HBJ Book
Harcourt Brace Jovanovich
New York and London

Copyright © 1943, 1971
by Harcourt Brace Jovanovich, Inc.

All rights reserved. No part of this publication may be
reproduced or transmitted in any form or by any means,
electronic or mechanical, including photocopy, record-
ing, or any information storage and retrieval system,
without permission in writing from the publisher.

Printed in the United States of America

Z

ISBN 0-15-246507-3

TO LEON WERTH

I ask the indulgence of the children who may read this book for dedicating it to a grown-up. I have a serious reason: he is the best friend I have in the world. I have another reason: this grown-up understands everything, even books about children. I have a third reason: he lives in France where he is hungry and cold. He needs cheering up. If all these reasons are not enough, I will dedicate the book to the child from whom this grown-up grew. All grown-ups were once children—although few of them remember it. And so I correct my dedication:

TO LEON WERTH
WHEN HE WAS A LITTLE BOY

The Little Prince

Once when I was six years old I saw a magnificent picture in a book, called *True Stories from Nature,* about the primeval forest. It was a picture of a boa constrictor in the act of swallowing an animal. Here is a copy of the drawing.

In the book it said: "Boa constrictors swallow their prey whole, without chewing it. After that they are not able to move, and they sleep through the six months that they need for digestion."

I pondered deeply, then, over the adventures of the jungle. And after some work with a colored pencil I succeeded in making my first drawing. My Drawing Number One. It looked like this:

I showed my masterpiece to the grown-ups, and asked them whether the drawing frightened them.

But they answered: "Frighten? Why should any one be frightened by a hat?"

My drawing was not a picture of a hat. It was a picture of a boa constrictor digesting an elephant. But since the grown-ups were not able to understand it, I made another drawing: I drew the inside of the boa constrictor, so that the grown-ups could see it clearly. They always need to have things explained. My Drawing Number Two looked like this:

The grown-ups' response, this time, was to advise me to lay aside my drawings of boa constrictors, whether from the inside or the outside, and devote myself instead to geography, history, arithmetic and grammar. That is why, at the age of six, I gave up what might have been a magnificent career as a painter. I had been disheartened by the failure of my Drawing Number One and my Drawing Number Two. Grown-ups never understand anything by themselves, and it is tiresome for children to be always and forever explaining things to them.

So then I chose another profession, and learned to pilot airplanes. I have flown a little over all parts of the world; and it is true that geography has been very useful to me. At a glance I can distinguish China from Arizona. If one gets lost in the night, such knowledge is valuable.

In the course of this life I have had a great many encounters with a great many people who have been concerned with matters of consequence. I have lived a great deal among grown-ups. I have seen them intimately, close at hand. And that hasn't much improved my opinion of them.

Whenever I met one of them who seemed to me at all clear-sighted, I tried the experiment of showing him my Drawing Number One, which I have always kept. I would try to find out, so, if this was a person of true understanding. But, whoever it was, he, or she, would always say:

"That is a hat."

Then I would never talk to that person about boa constrictors, or primeval forests, or stars. I would bring myself down to his level. I would talk to him about bridge, and golf, and politics, and neckties. And the grown-up would be greatly pleased to have met such a sensible man.

2

So I lived my life alone, without anyone that I could really talk to, until I had an accident with my plane in the Desert of Sahara, six years ago. Something was broken in my engine. And as I had with me neither a mechanic nor any passengers, I set myself to attempt the difficult repairs all alone. It was a question of life or death for me: I had scarcely enough drinking water to last a week.

The first night, then, I went to sleep on the sand, a thousand miles from any human habitation. I was more isolated than a shipwrecked sailor on a raft in the middle of the ocean. Thus you can imagine my amazement, at sunrise, when I was awakened by an odd little voice. It said:

"If you please—draw me a sheep!"

"What!"

"Draw me a sheep!"

I jumped to my feet, completely thunderstruck. I blinked my eyes hard. I looked carefully all around me. And I saw a most extraordinary small person, who stood there examining me with great seriousness. Here you may see the best portrait that, later, I was able to make of him. But my drawing is certainly very much less charming than its model.

That, however, is not my fault. The grown-ups discouraged me in my painter's career when I was six years old, and I never learned to draw anything, except boas from the outside and boas from the inside.

Now I stared at this sudden apparition with my eyes fairly starting out of my head in astonish-

"Here is the best portrait that, later, I was able to make of him."

ment. Remember, I had crashed in the desert a thousand miles from any inhabited region. And yet my little man seemed neither to be straying uncertainly among the sands, nor to be fainting from fatigue or hunger or thirst or fear. Nothing about him gave any suggestion of a child lost in the middle of the desert, a thousand miles from any human habitation. When at last I was able to speak, I said to him:

"But—what are you doing here?"

And in answer he repeated, very slowly, as if he were speaking of a matter of great consequence:

"If you please—draw me a sheep . . ."

When a mystery is too overpowering, one dare not disobey. Absurd as it might seem to me, a thousand miles from any human habitation and in danger of death, I took out of my pocket a sheet of paper and my fountain-pen. But then I remembered how my studies had been concentrated on geography, history, arithmetic and grammar, and I told the little chap (a little crossly, too) that I did not know how to draw. He answered me:

"That doesn't matter. Draw me a sheep . . ."

But I had never drawn a sheep. So I drew for him one of the two pictures I had drawn so often. It was that of the boa constrictor from the outside. And I was astounded to hear the little fellow greet it with,

"No, no, no! I do not want an elephant inside

a boa constrictor. A boa constrictor is a very dangerous creature, and an elephant is very cum-

bersome. Where I live, everything is very small. What I need is a sheep. Draw me a sheep."

So then I made a drawing.

He looked at it carefully, then he said:

"No. This sheep is already very sickly. Make me another."

So I made another drawing.

My friend smiled gently and indulgently.

"You see yourself," he said, "that this is not a sheep. This is a ram. It has horns."

So then I did my drawing over once more.

But it was rejected too, just like the others.

"This one is too old. I want a sheep that will live a long time."

By this time my patience was exhausted, because I was in a hurry to start taking my engine apart. So I tossed off this drawing.

And I threw out an explanation with it.

"This is only his box. The sheep you asked for is inside."

I was very surprised to see a light break over the face of my young judge:

"That is exactly the way I wanted it! Do you think that this sheep will have to have a great deal of grass?"

"Why?"

"Because where I live everything is very small . . ."

"There will surely be enough grass for him," I said. "It is a very small sheep that I have given you."

He bent his head over the drawing:

"Not so small that—Look! He has gone to sleep . . ."

And that is how I made the acquaintance of the little prince.

3

It took me a long time to learn where he came from. The little prince, who asked me so many questions, never seemed to hear the ones I asked him. It was from words dropped by chance that, little by little, everything was revealed to me.

The first time he saw my airplane, for instance (I shall not draw my airplane; that would be much too complicated for me), he asked me:

"What is that object?"

"That is not an object. It flies. It is an airplane. It is my airplane."

And I was proud to have him learn that I could fly.

He cried out, then:

"What! You dropped down from the sky?"

"Yes," I answered, modestly.

"Oh! That is funny!"

And the little prince broke into a lovely peal of laughter, which irritated me very much. I like my misfortunes to be taken seriously.

Then he added:

"So you, too, come from the sky! Which is your planet?"

At that moment I caught a gleam of light in the impenetrable mystery of his presence; and I demanded, abruptly:

"Do you come from another planet?"

But he did not reply. He tossed his head gently, without taking his eyes from my plane:

"It is true that on that you can't have come from very far away . . ."

And he sank into a reverie, which lasted a long time. Then, taking my sheep out of his pocket, he buried himself in the contemplation of his treasure.

You can imagine how my curiosity was aroused by this half-confidence about the "other planets." I made a great effort, therefore, to find out more on this subject.

"My little man, where do you come from? What is this 'where I live,' of which you speak? Where do you want to take your sheep?"

After a reflective silence he answered:

"The thing that is so good about the box you have given me is that at night he can use it as his house."

"That is so. And if you are good I will give you a string, too, so that you can tie him during the day, and a post to tie him to."

But the little prince seemed shocked by this offer:

"Tie him! What a queer idea!"

"But if you don't tie him," I said, "he will wander off somewhere, and get lost."

My friend broke into another peal of laughter:

"But where do you think he would go?"

"Anywhere. Straight ahead of him."

Then the little prince said, earnestly:

"That doesn't matter. Where I live, everything is so small!"

And, with perhaps a hint of sadness, he added:

"Straight ahead of him, nobody can go very far . . ."

The Little Prince on Asteroid B-612

4

I had thus learned a second fact of great importance: this was that the planet the little prince came from was scarcely any larger than a house!

But that did not really surprise me much. I knew very well that in addition to the great planets —such as the Earth, Jupiter, Mars, Venus—to which we have given names, there are also hundreds of others, some of which are so small that one has a hard time seeing them through the telescope. When an astronomer discovers one of these he does not give it a name, but only a number. He might call it, for example, "Asteroid 325."

I have serious reason to believe that the planet
from which the little prince came is the asteroid
known as B-612.

This asteroid has only once been seen through
the telescope. That was by a Turkish astronomer,
in 1909.

On making his discovery, the astronomer had
presented it to the International Astronomical
Congress, in a great demonstration. But he was
in Turkish costume, and so nobody would believe
what he said.

Grown-ups are like that . . .

Fortunately, however, for the reputation of
Asteroid B-612, a Turkish dictator made a law
that his subjects, under pain of death, should

change to European costume. So in 1920 the astronomer gave his demonstration all over again, dressed with impressive style and elegance. And this time everybody accepted his report.

If I have told you these details about the asteroid, and made a note of its number for you, it is on account of the grown-ups and their ways. Grownups love figures. When you tell them that you have made a new friend, they never ask you any questions about essential matters. They never say to you, "What does his voice sound like? What games does he love best? Does he collect butterflies?" Instead, they demand: "How old is he? How many brothers has he? How much does he weigh? How much money does his father make?"

Only from these figures do they think they have learned anything about him.

If you were to say to the grown-ups: "I saw a beautiful house made of rosy brick, with geraniums in the windows and doves on the roof," they would not be able to get any idea of that house at all. You would have to say to them: "I saw a house that cost $20,000." Then they would exclaim: "Oh, what a pretty house that is!"

Just so, you might say to them: "The proof that the little prince existed is that he was charming, that he laughed, and that he was looking for a sheep. If anybody wants a sheep, that is a proof that he exists." And what good would it do to tell them that? They would shrug their shoulders, and treat you like a child. But if you said to them: "The planet he came from is Asteroid B-612," then they would be convinced, and leave you in peace from their questions.

They are like that. One must not hold it against them. Children should always show great forbearance toward grown-up people.

But certainly, for us who understand life, figures are a matter of indifference. I should have liked to begin this story in the fashion of the fairy-tales. I should have liked to say: "Once upon a time there was a little prince who lived on a planet that was scarcely any bigger than himself, and who had need of a sheep . . ."

To those who understand life, that would have given a much greater air of truth to my story.

For I do not want any one to read my book carelessly. I have suffered too much grief in setting down these memories. Six years have already passed since my friend went away from me, with his sheep. If I try to describe him here, it is to make sure that I shall not forget him. To forget a friend is sad. Not every one has had a friend. And if I forget him, I may become like the grown-ups who are no longer interested in anything but figures . . .

It is for that purpose, again, that I have bought a box of paints and some pencils. It is hard to take up drawing again at my age, when I have never made any pictures except those of the boa constrictor from the outside and the boa constrictor from the inside, since I was six. I shall certainly try to make my portraits as true to life as possible. But I am not at all sure of success. One drawing goes along all right, and another has no resemblance to its subject. I make some errors, too, in the little prince's height: in one place he is too tall and in another too short. And I feel some doubts about the color of his costume. So I fumble along as best I can, now good, now bad, and I hope generally fair-to-middling.

In certain more important details I shall make mistakes, also. But that is something that will not be my fault. My friend never explained anything to me. He thought, perhaps, that I was like himself. But I, alas, do not know how to see sheep through the walls of boxes. Perhaps I am a little like the grown-ups. I have had to grow old.

5

As each day passed I would learn, in our talk, something about the little prince's planet, his departure from it, his journey. The information would come very slowly, as it might chance to fall from his thoughts. It was in this way that I heard, on the third day, about the catastrophe of the baobabs.

This time, once more, I had the sheep to thank for it. For the little prince asked me abruptly—as if seized by a grave doubt—"It is true, isn't it, that sheep eat little bushes?"

"Yes, that is true."

"Ah! I am glad!"

I did not understand why it was so important that sheep should eat little bushes. But the little prince added:

"Then it follows that they also eat baobabs?"

I pointed out to the little prince that baobabs were not little bushes, but, on the contrary, trees as big as castles; and that even if he took a whole herd of elephants away with him, the herd would not eat up one single baobab.

The idea of the herd of elephants made the little prince laugh.

"We would have to put them one on top of the other," he said.

But he made a wise comment:

"Before they grow so big, the baobabs start out by being little."

"That is strictly correct," I said. "But why do you want the sheep to eat the little baobabs?"

He answered me at once, "Oh, come, come!", as if he were speaking of something that was self-evident. And I was obliged to make a great mental effort to solve this problem, without any assistance.

Indeed, as I learned, there were on the planet where the little prince lived—as on all planets —good plants and bad plants. In consequence, there were good seeds from good plants, and bad seeds from bad plants. But seeds are invisible. They sleep deep in the heart of the earth's darkness, until some one among them is seized with the desire to awaken. Then this little seed will stretch itself and begin—timidly at first—to push a charming little sprig inoffensively upward toward the sun. If it is only a sprout of radish or the sprig of a rose-bush, one would let it grow wherever it might wish. But when it is a bad plant, one must destroy it as soon as possible, the very first instant that one recognizes it.

Now there were some terrible seeds on the planet that was the home of the little prince; and these were the seeds of the baobab. The soil of that planet was infested with them. A baobab is something you will never, never be able to get rid of if you attend to it too late. It spreads over the entire planet. It bores clear through it with its roots. And if the planet is too small, and the baobabs are too many, they split it in pieces . . .

"It is a question of discipline," the little prince said to me later on. "When you've finished your own toilet in the morning, then it is time to attend to the toilet of your planet, just so, with the greatest care. You must see to it that you pull up regularly all the baobabs, at the very first moment when they can be distinguished from the rose-bushes which they resemble so closely in their earliest youth. It is very tedious work," the little prince added, "but very easy."

And one day he said to me: "You ought to make a beautiful drawing, so that the children where you live can see exactly how all this is. That would be very useful to them if they were to travel some day. Sometimes," he added, "there is no harm in putting off a piece of work until another day. But when it is a matter of baobabs, that always means a catastrophe. I knew a planet that was inhabited by a lazy man. He neglected three little bushes . . ."

So, as the little prince described it to me, I have made a drawing of that planet. I do not much like to take the tone of a moralist. But the danger of the baobabs is so little understood, and such considerable risks would be run by anyone who might get lost on an asteroid, that for once I am breaking through my reserve. "Children," I say plainly, "watch out for the baobabs!"

My friends, like myself, have been skirting this danger for a long time, without ever knowing it; and so it is for them that I have worked so hard over this drawing. The lesson which I pass on by this means is worth all the trouble it has cost me.

Perhaps you will ask me, "Why are there no other drawings in this book as magnificent and impressive as this drawing of the baobabs?"

The reply is simple. I have tried. But with the others I have not been successful. When I made the drawing of the baobabs I was carried beyond myself by the inspiring force of urgent necessity.

6

Oh, little prince! Bit by bit I came to understand the secrets of your sad little life . . . For a long time you had found your only entertainment in the quiet pleasure of looking at the sunset. I learned that new detail on the morning of the fourth day, when you said to me:

"I am very fond of sunsets. Come, let us go look at a sunset now."

"But we must wait," I said.

"Wait? For what?"

"For the sunset. We must wait until it is time."

At first you seemed to be very much surprised. And then you laughed to yourself. You said to me:

"I am always thinking that I am at home!"

Just so. Everybody knows that when it is noon in the United States the sun is setting over France.

The Baobabs

If you could fly to France in one minute, you could go straight into the sunset, right from noon. Unfortunately, France is too far away for that. But on your tiny planet, my little prince, all you need do is move your chair a few steps. You can see the day end and the twilight falling whenever you like . . .

"One day," you said to me, "I saw the sunset forty-four times!"

And a little later you added:

"You know—one loves the sunset, when one is so sad . . ."

"Were you so sad, then?" I asked, "on the day of the forty-four sunsets?"

But the little prince made no reply.

7

On the fifth day—again, as always, it was thanks to the sheep—the secret of the little prince's life was revealed to me. Abruptly, without anything to lead up to it, and as if the question had been born of long and silent meditation on his problem, he demanded:

"A sheep—if it eats little bushes, does it eat flowers, too?"

"A sheep," I answered, "eats anything it finds in its reach."

"Even flowers that have thorns?"

"Yes, even flowers that have thorns."

"Then the thorns—what use are they?"

I did not know. At that moment I was very busy trying to unscrew a bolt that had got stuck in my engine. I was very much worried, for it was becoming clear to me that the breakdown of my plane was extremely serious. And I had so little drinking-water left that I had to fear the worst.

"The thorns—what use are they?"

The little prince never let go of a question, once he had asked it. As for me, I was upset over that bolt. And I answered with the first thing that came into my head:

"The thorns are of no use at all. Flowers have thorns just for spite!"

"Oh!"

There was a moment of complete silence. Then the little prince flashed back at me, with a kind of resentfulness:

"I don't believe you! Flowers are weak creatures. They are naïve. They reassure themselves as best they can. They believe that their thorns are terrible weapons . . ."

I did not answer. At that instant I was saying to myself: "If this bolt still won't turn, I am going to knock it out with the hammer." Again the little prince disturbed my thoughts:

"And you actually believe that the flowers—"

"Oh, no!" I cried. "No, no, no! I don't believe anything. I answered you with the first thing that came into my head. Don't you see—I am very busy with matters of consequence!"

He stared at me, thunderstruck.

"Matters of consequence!"

He looked at me there, with my hammer in my hand, my fingers black with engine-grease, bending down over an object which seemed to him extremely ugly . . .

"You talk just like the grown-ups!"

That made me a little ashamed. But he went on, relentlessly:

"You mix everything up together . . . You confuse everything . . ."

He was really very angry. He tossed his golden curls in the breeze.

"I know a planet where there is a certain red-faced gentleman. He has never smelled a flower. He has never looked at a star. He has never loved any one. He has never done anything in his life but add up figures. And all day he says over and over, just like you: 'I am busy with matters of consequence!' And that makes him swell up with pride. But he is not a man—he is a mushroom!"

"A what?"

"A mushroom!"

The little prince was now white with rage.

"The flowers have been growing thorns for millions of years. For millions of years the sheep have been eating them just the same. And is it not a matter of consequence to try to understand why the flowers go to so much trouble to grow thorns which are never of any use to them? Is the warfare between the sheep and the flowers not important? Is this not of more consequence than a fat red-faced gentleman's sums? And if I know —I, myself—one flower which is unique in the world, which grows nowhere but on my planet, but which one little sheep can destroy in a single bite some morning, without even noticing what he is doing—Oh! You think that is not important!"

His face turned from white to red as he continued:

"If some one loves a flower, of which just one

single blossom grows in all the millions and millions of stars, it is enough to make him happy just to look at the stars. He can say to himself: 'Somewhere, my flower is there . . .' But if the sheep eats the flower, in one moment all his stars will be darkened . . . And you think that is not important!"

He could not say anything more. His words were choked by sobbing.

The night had fallen. I had let my tools drop from my hands. Of what moment now was my hammer, my bolt, or thirst, or death? On one star, one planet, my planet, the Earth, there was a little prince to be comforted. I took him in my arms, and rocked him. I said to him:

"The flower that you love is not in danger. I will draw you a muzzle for your sheep. I will draw you a railing to put around your flower. I will—"

I did not know what to say to him. I felt awkward and blundering. I did not know how I could reach him, where I could overtake him and go on hand in hand with him once more.

It is such a secret place, the land of tears.

8

I soon learned to know this flower better. On the little prince's planet the flowers had always been very simple. They had only one ring of petals; they took up no room at all; they were a trouble to nobody. One morning they would appear in the grass, and by night they would have faded peacefully away. But one day, from a seed blown from no one knew where, a new flower had come up; and the little prince had watched very closely over this small sprout which was not like any other small sprouts on his planet. It might, you see, have been a new kind of baobab.

But the shrub soon stopped growing, and began to get ready to produce a flower. The little prince, who was present at the first appearance of a huge bud, felt at once that some sort of miraculous apparition must emerge from it. But the flower was not satisfied to complete the preparations for her beauty in the shelter of her green chamber. She chose her colors with the greatest care. She dressed herself slowly. She adjusted her petals one by one. She did not wish to go out into the world all rumpled, like the field poppies. It was only in the full radiance of her beauty that she wished to appear. Oh, yes! She was a coquettish creature! And her mysterious adornment lasted for days and days.

Then one morning, exactly at sunrise, she suddenly showed herself.

And, after working with all this painstaking precision, she yawned and said:

"Ah! I am scarcely awake. I beg that you will excuse me. My petals are still all disarranged . . ."

But the little prince could not restrain his admiration:

"Oh! How beautiful you are!"

"Am I not?" the flower responded, sweetly. "And I was born at the same moment as the sun . . ."

The little prince could guess easily enough that she was not any too modest—but how moving—and exciting—she was!

"I think it is time for breakfast," she added an instant later. "If you would have the kindness to think of my needs—"

And the little prince, completely abashed, went to look for a sprinkling-can of fresh water. So, he tended the flower.

So, too, she began very quickly to torment him with her vanity—which was, if the truth be known, a little difficult to deal with. One day, for instance, when she was speaking of her four thorns, she said to the little prince:

"Let the tigers come with their claws!"

"There are no tigers on my planet," the little prince objected. "And, anyway, tigers do not eat weeds."

"I am not a weed," the flower replied, sweetly.

"Please excuse me . . ."

"I am not at all afraid of tigers," she went on, "but I have a horror of drafts. I suppose you wouldn't have a screen for me?"

"A horror of drafts—that is bad luck, for a plant," remarked the little prince, and added to himself, "This flower is a very complex creature . . ."

"At night I want you to put me under a glass globe. It is very cold where you live. In the place I came from—"

But she interrupted herself at that point. She had come in the form of a seed. She could not have known anything of any other worlds. Embarrassed over having let herself be caught on the verge of such a naïve untruth, she coughed two or three times, in order to put the little prince in the wrong.

"The screen?"

"I was just going to look for it when you spoke to me . . ."

Then she forced her cough a little more so that he should suffer from remorse just the same.

So the little prince, in spite of all the good will that was inseparable from his love, had soon come to doubt her. He had taken seriously words which were without importance, and it made him very unhappy.

"I ought not to have listened to her," he confided to me one day. "One never ought to listen to the flowers. One should simply look at them and breathe their fragrance. Mine perfumed all my planet. But I did not know how to take pleasure in all her grace. This tale of claws, which disturbed me so much, should only have filled my heart with tenderness and pity."

And he continued his confidences:

"The fact is that I did not know how to understand anything! I ought to have judged by deeds and not by words. She cast her fragrance and her radiance over me. I ought never to have run away from her . . . I ought to have guessed all the affection that lay behind her poor little stratagems. Flowers are so inconsistent! But I was too young to know how to love her . . ."

9

I believe that for his escape he took advantage of the migration of a flock of wild birds. On the morning of his departure he put his planet in perfect order. He carefully cleaned out his active volcanoes. He possessed two active volcanoes; and they were very convenient for heating his breakfast in the morning. He also had one volcano that was extinct. But, as he said, "One never knows!" So he cleaned out the extinct volcano, too. If they are well cleaned out, volcanoes burn slowly and steadily, without any eruptions. Volcanic eruptions are like fires in a chimney.

On our earth we are obviously much too small to clean out our volcanoes. That is why they bring no end of trouble upon us.

The little prince also pulled up, with a certain sense of dejection, the last little shoots of the baobabs. He believed that he would never want to return. But on this last morning all these familiar tasks seemed very precious to him. And when he watered the flower for the last time, and prepared to place her under the shelter of her glass globe, he realized that he was very close to tears.

"Goodbye," he said to the flower.

But she made no answer.

"Goodbye," he said again.

"He carefully cleaned out his active volcanoes."

The flower coughed. But it was not because she had a cold.

"I have been silly," she said to him, at last. "I ask your forgiveness. Try to be happy . . ."

He was surprised by this absence of reproaches. He stood there all bewildered, the glass globe held arrested in mid-air. He did not understand this quiet sweetness.

"Of course I love you," the flower said to him. "It is my fault that you have not known it all the while. That is of no importance. But you—you have been just as foolish as I. Try to be happy . . . Let the glass globe be. I don't want it any more."

"But the wind—"

"My cold is not so bad as all that . . . The cool night air will do me good. I am a flower."

"But the animals—"

"Well, I must endure the presence of two or three caterpillars if I wish to become acquainted with the butterflies. It seems that they are very beautiful. And if not the butterflies—and the caterpillars—who will call upon me? You will be far away . . . As for the large animals—I am not at all afraid of any of them. I have my claws."

And, naïvely, she showed her four thorns. Then she added:

"Don't linger like this. You have decided to go away. Now go!"

For she did not want him to see her crying. She was such a proud flower . . .

He found himself in the neighborhood of the asteroids 325, 326, 327, 328, 329, and 330. He began, therefore, by visiting them, in order to add to his knowledge.

The first of them was inhabited by a king. Clad in royal purple and ermine, he was seated upon a throne which was at the same time both simple and majestic.

"Ah! Here is a subject," exclaimed the king, when he saw the little prince coming.

And the little prince asked himself:

"How could he recognize me when he had never seen me before?"

He did not know how the world is simplified for kings. To them, all men are subjects.

"Approach, so that I may see you better," said the king, who felt consumingly proud of being at last a king over somebody.

The little prince looked everywhere to find a place to sit down; but the entire planet was crammed and obstructed by the king's magnificent ermine robe. So he remained standing upright, and, since he was tired, he yawned.

"It is contrary to etiquette to yawn in the presence of a king," the monarch said to him. "I forbid you to do so."

"I can't help it. I can't stop myself," replied the little prince, thoroughly embarrassed. "I have come on a long journey, and I have had no sleep . . ."

"Ah, then," the king said. "I order you to yawn. It is years since I have seen anyone yawning. Yawns, to me, are objects of curiosity. Come, now! Yawn again! It is an order."

"That frightens me . . . I cannot, any more . . ." murmured the little prince, now completely abashed.

"Hum! Hum!" replied the king. "Then I—I order you sometimes to yawn and sometimes to—"

He sputtered a little, and seemed vexed.

For what the king fundamentally insisted upon was that his authority should be respected. He tolerated no disobedience. He was an absolute monarch. But, because he was a very good man, he made his orders reasonable.

"If I ordered a general," he would say, by way of example, "if I ordered a general to change himself into a sea bird, and if the general did not obey me, that would not be the fault of the general. It would be my fault."

"May I sit down?" came now a timid inquiry from the little prince.

"I order you to do so," the king answered him, and majestically gathered in a fold of his ermine mantle.

But the little prince was wondering . . . The

". . . the entire planet was crammed and obstructed
by the king's magnificent ermine robe."

planet was tiny. Over what could this king really rule?

"Sire," he said to him, "I beg that you will excuse my asking you a question—"

"I order you to ask me a question," the king hastened to assure him.

"Sire—over what do you rule?"

"Over everything," said the king, with magnificent simplicity.

"Over everything?"

The king made a gesture, which took in his planet, the other planets, and all the stars.

"Over all that?" asked the little prince.

"Over all that," the king answered.

For his rule was not only absolute: it was also univeral.

"And the stars obey you?"

"Certainly they do," the king said. "They obey instantly. I do not permit insubordination."

Such power was a thing for the little prince to marvel at. If he had been master of such complete authority, he would have been able to watch the sunset, not forty-four times in one day, but seventy-two, or even a hundred, or even two hundred times, without ever having to move his chair. And because he felt a bit sad as he remembered his little planet which he had forsaken, he plucked up his courage to ask the king a favor:

"I should like to see a sunset . . . Do me that kindness . . . Order the sun to set . . ."

"If I ordered a general to fly from one flower to another like a butterfly, or to write a tragic drama, or to change himself into a sea bird, and if the general did not carry out the order that he had received, which one of us would be in the wrong?" the king demanded. "The general, or myself?"

"You," said the little prince firmly.

"Exactly. One must require from each one the duty which each one can perform," the king went on. "Accepted authority rests first of all on reason. If you ordered your people to go and throw themselves into the sea, they would rise up in revolution. I have the right to require obedience because my orders are reasonable."

"Then my sunset?" the little prince reminded him: for he never forgot a question once he had asked it.

"You shall have your sunset. I shall command it. But, according to my science of government, I shall wait until conditions are favorable."

"When will that be?" inquired the little prince.

"Hum! Hum!" replied the king; and before saying anything else he consulted a bulky almanac. "Hum! Hum! That will be about—about —that will be this evening about twenty minutes to eight. And you will see how well I am obeyed!"

The little prince yawned. He was regretting his lost sunset. And then, too, he was already beginning to be a little bored.

"I have nothing more to do here," he said to the king. "So I shall set out on my way again."

"Do not go," said the king, who was very proud of having a subject. "Do not go. I will make you a Minister!"

"Minister of what?"

"Minister of—of Justice!"

"But there is nobody here to judge!"

"We do not know that," the king said to him. "I have not yet made a complete tour of my kingdom. I am very old. There is no room here for a carriage. And it tires me to walk."

"Oh, but I have looked already!" said the little prince, turning around to give one more glance to the other side of the planet. On that side, as on this, there was nobody at all . . .

"Then you shall judge yourself," the king answered. "That is the most difficult thing of all. It is much more difficult to judge oneself than to judge others. If you succeed in judging yourself rightly, then you are indeed a man of true wisdom."

"Yes," said the little prince, "but I can judge myself anywhere. I do not need to live on this planet."

"Hum! Hum!" said the king. "I have good reason to believe that somewhere on my planet there is an old rat. I hear him at night. You can judge this old rat. From time to time you will condemn him to death. Thus his life will depend on your justice. But you will pardon him on each occasion; for he must be treated thriftily. He is the only one we have."

"I," replied the little prince, "do not like to condemn anyone to death. And now I think I will go on my way."

"No," said the king.

But the little prince, having now completed his preparations for departure, had no wish to grieve the old monarch.

"If Your Majesty wishes to be promptly obeyed," he said, "he should be able to give me a reasonable order. He should be able, for example, to order me to be gone by the end of one minute. It seems to me that conditions are favorable . . ."

As the king made no answer, the little prince hesitated a moment. Then, with a sigh, he took his leave.

"I make you my Ambassador," the king called out, hastily.

He had a magnificent air of authority.

"The grown-ups are very strange," the little prince said to himself, as he continued on his journey.

II

The second planet was inhabited by a conceited man.

"Ah! Ah! I am about to receive a visit from an

admirer!" he exclaimed from afar, when he first saw the little prince coming.

For, to conceited men, all other men are admirers.

"Good morning," said the little prince. "That is a queer hat you are wearing."

"It is a hat for salutes," the conceited man replied. "It is to raise in salute when people acclaim me. Unfortunately, nobody at all ever passes this way."

"Yes?" said the little prince, who did not understand what the conceited man was talking about.

"Clap your hands, one against the other," the conceited man now directed him.

The little prince clapped his hands. The conceited man raised his hat in a modest salute.

"This is more entertaining than the visit to the king," the little prince said to himself. And he began again to clap his hands, one against the other. The conceited man again raised his hat in salute.

After five minutes of this exercise the little prince grew tired of the game's monotony.

"And what should one do to make the hat come down?" he asked.

But the conceited man did not hear him. Conceited people never hear anything but praise.

"Do you really admire me very much?" he demanded of the little prince.

"What does that mean—'admire'?"

*"Ah! Ah! I am about to receive a visit
from an admirer!"*

"To admire means that you regard me as the handsomest, the best-dressed, the richest, and the most intelligent man on this planet."

"But you are the only man on your planet!"

"Do me this kindness. Admire me just the same."

"I admire you," said the little prince, shrugging his shoulders slightly, "but what is there in that to interest you so much?"

And the little prince went away.

"The grown-ups are certainly very odd," he said to himself, as he continued on his journey.

12

The next planet was inhabited by a tippler. This was a very short visit, but it plunged the little prince into deep dejection.

"What are you doing there?" he said to the tippler, whom he found settled down in silence before a collection of empty bottles and also a collection of full bottles.

"I am drinking," replied the tippler, with a lugubrious air.

"Why are you drinking?" demanded the little prince.

"So that I may forget," replied the tippler.

"Forget what?" inquired the little prince, who already was sorry for him.

"The next planet was inhabited by a tippler."

"Forget that I am ashamed," the tippler confessed, hanging his head.

"Ashamed of what?" insisted the little prince, who wanted to help him.

"Ashamed of drinking!" The tippler brought his speech to an end, and shut himself up in an impregnable silence.

And the little prince went away, puzzled.

"The grown-ups are certainly very, very odd," he said to himself, as he continued on his journey.

13

The fourth planet belonged to a businessman. This man was so much occupied that he did not even raise his head at the little prince's arrival.

"Good morning," the little prince said to him. "Your cigarette has gone out."

"Three and two make five. Five and seven make twelve. Twelve and three make fifteen. Good morning. Fifteen and seven make twenty-two. Twenty-two and six make twenty-eight. I haven't time to light it again. Twenty-six and five make thirty-one. Phew! Then that makes five-hundred-and-one million, six-hundred-twenty-two thousand, seven-hundred-thirty-one."

"Five hundred million what?" asked the little prince.

"Eh? Are you still there? Five-hundred-and-one million—I can't stop . . . I have so much to do! I am concerned with matters of consequence. I don't amuse myself with balderdash. Two and five make seven . . ."

"Five-hundred-and-one million what?" repeated the little prince, who never in his life had let go of a question once he had asked it.

The businessman raised his head.

"During the fifty-four years that I have inhabited this planet, I have been disturbed only three times. The first time was twenty-two years ago, when some giddy goose fell from goodness knows where. He made the most frightful noise that resounded all over the place, and I made four mistakes in my addition. The second time, eleven years ago, I was disturbed by an attack of rheumatism. I don't get enough exercise. I have no time for loafing. The third time—well, this is it! I was saying, then, five-hundred-and-one millions—"

"Millions of what?"

The businessman suddenly realized that there was no hope of being left in peace until he answered this question.

"Millions of those little objects," he said, "which one sometimes sees in the sky."

"Flies?"

"Oh, no. Little glittering objects."

"Bees?"

"Oh, no. Little golden objects that set lazy men to idle dreaming. As for me, I am concerned with matters of consequence. There is no time for idle dreaming in my life."

"Ah! You mean the stars?"

"Yes, that's it. The stars."

"And what do you do with five-hundred millions of stars?"

"Five-hundred-and-one million, six-hundred-
twenty-two thousand, seven-hundred-thirty-one.
I am concerned with matters of consequence: I
am accurate."

"And what do you do with these stars?"

"What do I do with them?"

"Yes."

"Nothing. I own them."

"You own the stars?"

"Yes."

"But I have already seen a king who—"

"Kings do not *own,* they *reign over.* It is a very
different matter."

"And what good does it do you to own the
stars?"

"It does me the good of making me rich."

"And what good does it do you to be rich?"

"It makes it possible for me to buy more stars,
if any are discovered."

"This man," the little prince said to himself,
"reasons a little like my poor tippler . . ."

Nevertheless, he still had some more questions.

"How is it possible for one to own the stars?"

"To whom do they belong?" the businessman
retorted, peevishly.

"I don't know. To nobody."

"Then they belong to me, because I was the
first person to think of it."

"Is that all that is necessary?"

"Certainly. When you find a diamond that belongs to nobody, it is yours. When you discover an island that belongs to nobody, it is yours. When you get an idea before any one else, you take out a patent on it: it is yours. So with me: I own the stars, because nobody else before me ever thought of owning them."

"Yes, that is true," said the little prince. "And what do you do with them?"

"I administer them," replied the businessman. "I count them and recount them. It is difficult. But I am a man who is naturally interested in matters of consequence."

The little prince was still not satisfied.

"If I owned a silk scarf," he said, "I could put it around my neck and take it away with me. If I owned a flower, I could pluck that flower and take it away with me. But you cannot pluck the stars from heaven . . ."

"No. But I can put them in the bank."

"Whatever does that mean?"

"That means that I write the number of my stars on a little paper. And then I put this paper in a drawer and lock it with a key."

"And that is all?"

"That is enough," said the businessman.

"It is entertaining," thought the little prince. "It is rather poetic. But it is of no great consequence."

On matters of consequence, the little prince

had ideas which were very different from those of the grown-ups.

"I myself own a flower," he continued his conversation with the businessman, "which I water every day. I own three volcanoes, which I clean out every week (for I also clean out the one that is extinct; one never knows). It is of some use to my volcanoes, and it is of some use to my flower, that I own them. But you are of no use to the stars . . ."

The businessman opened his mouth, but he found nothing to say in answer. And the little prince went away.

"The grown-ups are certainly altogether extraordinary," he said simply, talking to himself as he continued on his journey.

14

The fifth planet was very strange. It was the smallest of all. There was just enough room on it for a street lamp and a lamplighter. The little prince was not able to reach any explanation of the use of a street lamp and a lamplighter, somewhere in the heavens, on a planet which had no people, and not one house. But he said to himself, nevertheless:

"It may well be that this man is absurd. But he

"I follow a terrible profession."

is not so absurd as the king, the conceited man, the businessman, and the tippler. For at least his work has some meaning. When he lights his street lamp, it is as if he brought one more star to life, or one flower. When he puts out his lamp, he sends the flower, or the star, to sleep. That is a beautiful occupation. And since it is beautiful, it is truly useful."

When he arrived on the planet he respectfully saluted the lamplighter.

"Good morning. Why have you just put out your lamp?"

"Those are the orders," replied the lamplighter. "Good morning."

"What are the orders?"

"The orders are that I put out my lamp. Good evening."

And he lighted his lamp again.

"But why have you just lighted it again?"

"Those are the orders," replied the lamplighter.

"I do not understand," said the little prince.

"There is nothing to understand," said the lamplighter. "Orders are orders. Good morning."

And he put out his lamp.

Then he mopped his forehead with a handkerchief decorated with red squares.

"I follow a terrible profession. In the old days it was reasonable. I put the lamp out in the morning, and in the evening I lighted it again. I had the rest of the day for relaxation and the rest of the night for sleep."

"And the orders have been changed since that time?"

"The orders have not been changed," said the lamplighter. "That is the tragedy! From year to year the planet has turned more rapidly and the orders have not been changed!"

"Then what?" asked the little prince.

"Then—the planet now makes a complete turn every minute, and I no longer have a single second for repose. Once every minute I have to light my lamp and put it out!"

"That is very funny! A day lasts only one minute, here where you live!"

"It is not funny at all!" said the lamplighter. "While we have been talking together a month has gone by."

"A month?"

"Yes, a month. Thirty minutes. Thirty days. Good evening."

And he lighted his lamp again.

As the little prince watched him, he felt that he loved this lamplighter who was so faithful to his orders. He remembered the sunsets which he himself had gone to seek, in other days, merely by pulling up his chair; and he wanted to help his friend.

"You know," he said, "I can tell you a way you can rest whenever you want to . . ."

"I always want to rest," said the lamplighter.

For it is possible for a man to be faithful and lazy at the same time.

The little prince went on with his explanation:

"Your planet is so small that three strides will take you all the way around it. To be always in the sunshine, you need only walk along rather slowly. When you want to rest, you will walk— and the day will last as long as you like."

"That doesn't do me much good," said the lamplighter. "The one thing I love in life is to sleep."

"Then you're unlucky," said the little prince.

"I am unlucky," said the lamplighter. "Good morning."

And he put out his lamp.

"That man," said the little prince to himself, as he continued farther on his journey, "that man would be scorned by all the others: by the king, by the conceited man, by the tippler, by the businessman. Nevertheless he is the only one of them all who does not seem to me ridiculous. Perhaps that is because he is thinking of something else besides himself."

He breathed a sigh of regret, and said to himself, again:

"That man is the only one of them all whom I could have made my friend. But his planet is indeed too small. There is no room on it for two people . . ."

What the little prince did not dare confess

was that he was sorry most of all to leave this planet, because it was blest every day with 1440 sunsets!

15

The sixth planet was ten times larger than the last one. It was inhabited by an old gentleman who wrote voluminous books.

"Oh, look! Here is an explorer!" he exclaimed to himself when he saw the little prince coming.

The little prince sat down on the table and panted a little. He had already traveled so much and so far!

"Where do you come from?" the old gentleman said to him.

"What is that big book?" said the little prince. "What are you doing?"

"I am a geographer," said the old gentleman.

"What is a geographer?" asked the little prince.

"A geographer is a scholar who knows the location of all the seas, rivers, towns, mountains, and deserts."

"That is very interesting," said the little prince. "Here at last is a man who has a real profession!" And he cast a look around him at the planet of the geographer. It was the most magnificent and stately planet that he had ever seen.

"Your planet is very beautiful," he said. "Has it any oceans?"

"I couldn't tell you," said the geographer.

"Ah!" The little prince was disappointed. "Has it any mountains?"

"I couldn't tell you," said the geographer.

"And towns, and rivers, and deserts?"

"I couldn't tell you that, either."

"But you are a geographer!"

"Exactly," the geographer said. "But I am not

an explorer. I haven't a single explorer on my planet. It is not the geographer who goes out to count the towns, the rivers, the mountains, the seas, the oceans, and the deserts. The geographer is much too important to go loafing about. He does not leave his desk. But he receives the explorers in his study. He asks them questions, and he notes down what they recall of their travels. And if the recollections of any one among them seem interesting to him, the geographer orders an inquiry into that explorer's moral character."

"Why is that?"

"Because an explorer who told lies would bring disaster on the books of the geographer. So would an explorer who drank too much."

"Why is that?" asked the little prince.

"Because intoxicated men see double. Then the geographer would note down two mountains in a place where there was only one."

"I know some one," said the little prince, "who would make a bad explorer."

"That is possible. Then, when the moral character of the explorer is shown to be good, an inquiry is ordered into his discovery."

"One goes to see it?"

"No. That would be too complicated. But one requires the explorer to furnish proofs. For example, if the discovery in question is that of a large mountain, one requires that large stones be brought back from it."

The geographer was suddenly stirred to excitement.

"But you—you come from far away! You are an explorer! You shall describe your planet to me!"

And, having opened his big register, the geographer sharpened his pencil. The recitals of explorers are put down first in pencil. One waits until the explorer has furnished proofs, before putting them down in ink.

"Well?" said the geographer expectantly.

"Oh, where I live," said the little prince, "it is not very interesting. It is all so small. I have three volcanoes. Two volcanoes are active and the other is extinct. But one never knows."

"One never knows," said the geographer.

"I have also a flower."

"We do not record flowers," said the geographer.

"Why is that? The flower is the most beautiful thing on my planet!"

"We do not record them," said the geographer, "because they are ephemeral."

"What does that mean—'ephemeral'?"

"Geographies," said the geographer, "are the books which, of all books, are most concerned with matters of consequence. They never become old-fashioned. It is very rarely that a mountain changes its position. It is very rarely that an ocean empties itself of its waters. We write of eternal things."

"But extinct volcanoes may come to life again," the little prince interrupted. "What does that mean—'ephemeral'?"

"Whether volcanoes are extinct or alive, it comes to the same thing for us," said the geographer. "The thing that matters to us is the mountain. It does not change."

"But what does that mean—'ephemeral'?" repeated the little prince, who never in his life had let go of a question, once he had asked it.

"It means, 'which is in danger of speedy disappearance.' "

"Is my flower in danger of speedy disappearance?"

"Certainly it is."

"My flower is ephemeral," the little prince said to himself, "and she has only four thorns to defend herself against the world. And I have left her on my planet, all alone!"

That was his first moment of regret. But he took courage once more.

"What place would you advise me to visit now?" he asked.

"The planet Earth," replied the geographer. "It has a good reputation."

And the little prince went away, thinking of his flower.

16

So then the seventh planet was the Earth.

The Earth is not just an ordinary planet! One can count, there, 111 kings (not forgetting, to be sure, the Negro kings among them), 7000 geographers, 900,000 businessmen, 7,500,000 tipplers, 311,000,000 conceited men—that is to say, about 2,000,000,000 grown-ups.

To give you an idea of the size of the Earth, I will tell you that before the invention of electricity it was necessary to maintain, over the whole of the six continents, a veritable army of 462,511 lamplighters for the street lamps.

Seen from a slight distance, that would make a splendid spectacle. The movements of this army would be regulated like those of the ballet in the opera. First would come the turn of the lamplighters of New Zealand and Australia. Having set their lamps alight, these would go off to sleep. Next, the lamplighters of China and Siberia would enter for their steps in the dance, and then they too would be waved back into the wings. After that would come the turn of the lamplighters of Russia and the Indies; then those of Africa and Europe; then those of South America; then those of North America. And never would they make a mistake in the order of their entry upon the stage. It would be magnificent.

Only the man who was in charge of the single lamp at the North Pole, and his colleague who was responsible for the single lamp at the South Pole— only these two would live free from toil and care: they would be busy twice a year.

17

When one wishes to play the wit, he sometimes wanders a little from the truth. I have not been altogether honest in what I have told you about the lamplighters. And I realize that I run the risk of giving a false idea of our planet to those who do not know it. Men occupy a very small place upon the Earth. If the two billion inhabitants who people its surface were all to stand upright and somewhat crowded together, as they do for some big public assembly, they could easily be put into one public square twenty miles long and twenty miles wide. All humanity could be piled up on a small Pacific islet.

The grown-ups, to be sure, will not believe you when you tell them that. They imagine that they fill a great deal of space. They fancy themselves as important as the baobabs. You should advise them, then, to make their own calculations. They adore figures, and that will please them. But do

*"When the little prince arrived on the Earth, he was
very surprised not to see any people."*

not waste your time on this extra task. It is unnecessary. You have, I know, confidence in me.

When the little prince arrived on the Earth, he was very much surprised not to see any people. He was beginning to be afraid he had come to the wrong planet, when a coil of gold, the color of the moonlight, flashed across the sand.

"Good evening," said the little prince courteously.

"Good evening," said the snake.

"What planet is this on which I have come down?" asked the little prince.

"This is the Earth; this is Africa," the snake answered.

"Ah! Then there are no people on the Earth?"

"This is the desert. There are no people in the desert. The Earth is large," said the snake.

The little prince sat down on a stone, and raised his eyes toward the sky.

"I wonder," he said, "whether the stars are set alight in heaven so that one day each one of us may find his own again . . . Look at my planet. It is right there above us. But how far away it is!"

"It is beautiful," the snake said. "What has brought you here?"

"I have been having some trouble with a flower," said the little prince.

"Ah!" said the snake.

And they were both silent.

"Where are the men?" the little prince at last

*"You are a funny animal . . . You are no thicker
than a finger."*

took up the conversation again. "It is a little lonely in the desert . . ."

"It is also lonely among men," the snake said.

The little prince gazed at him for a long time.

"You are a funny animal," he said at last. "You are no thicker than a finger . . ."

"But I am more powerful than the finger of a king," said the snake.

The little prince smiled.

"You are not very powerful. You haven't even any feet. You cannot even travel . . ."

"I can carry you farther than any ship could take you," said the snake.

He twined himself around the little prince's ankle, like a golden bracelet.

"Whomever I touch, I send back to the earth from whence he came," the snake spoke again. "But you are innocent and true, and you come from a star . . ."

The little prince made no reply.

"You move me to pity—you are so weak on this Earth made of granite," the snake said. "I can help you, some day, if you grow too homesick for your own planet. I can—"

"Oh! I understand you very well," said the little prince. "But why do you always speak in riddles?"

"I solve them all," said the snake.

And they were both silent.

18

The little prince crossed the desert and met with only one flower. It was a flower with three petals, a flower of no account at all.

"Good morning," said the little prince.

"Good morning," said the flower.

"Where are the men?" the little prince asked, politely.

The flower had once seen a caravan passing.

"Men?" she echoed. "I think there are six or seven of them in existence. I saw them, several years ago. But one never knows where to find them. The wind blows them away. They have no roots, and that makes their life very difficult."

"Goodbye," said the little prince.

"Goodbye," said the flower.

19

After that, the little prince climbed a high mountain. The only mountains he had ever known were the three volcanoes, which came up to his

"This planet is altogether dry, and altogether pointed."

knees. And he used the extinct volcano as a foot-stool. "From a mountain as high as this one," he said to himself, "I shall be able to see the whole planet at one glance, and all the people . . ."

But he saw nothing, save peaks of rock that were sharpened like needles.

"Good morning," he said courteously.

"Good morning—Good morning—Good morning," answered the echo.

"Who are you?" said the little prince.

"Who are you—Who are you—Who are you?" answered the echo.

"Be my friends. I am all alone," he said.

"I am all alone—all alone—all alone," answered the echo.

"What a queer planet!" he thought. "It is altogether dry, and altogether pointed, and altogether harsh and forbidding. And the people have no imagination. They repeat whatever one says to them . . . On my planet I had a flower; she always was the first to speak . . ."

20

But it happened that after walking for a long time through sand, and rocks, and snow, the little prince at last came upon a road. And all roads lead to the abodes of men.

"Good morning," he said.

He was standing before a garden, all a-bloom with roses.

"Good morning," said the roses.

The little prince gazed at them. They all looked like his flower.

"Who are you?" he demanded, thunderstruck.

"We are roses," the roses said.

And he was overcome with sadness. His flower had told him that she was the only one of her kind in all the universe. And here were five thousand of them, all alike, in one single garden!

"She would be very much annoyed," he said to himself, "if she should see that . . . She would cough most dreadfully, and she would pretend that she was dying, to avoid being laughed at. And I should be obliged to pretend that I was nursing her back to life—for if I did not do that, to humble myself also, she would really allow herself to die . . ."

Then he went on with his reflections: "I thought that I was rich, with a flower that was unique in all the world; and all I had was a common rose. A common rose, and three volcanoes that come up to my knees—and one of them perhaps extinct forever . . . That doesn't make me a very great prince . . ."

And he lay down in the grass and cried.

21

It was then that the fox appeared.

"Good morning," said the fox.

"Good morning," the little prince responded politely, although when he turned around he saw nothing.

"I am right here," the voice said, "under the apple tree."

"Who are you?" asked the little prince, and added, "You are very pretty to look at."

"I am a fox," the fox said.

"Come and play with me," proposed the little prince. "I am so unhappy."

"And he lay down on the grass and cried."

"I cannot play with you," the fox said. "I am not tamed."

"Ah! Please excuse me," said the little prince.

But, after some thought, he added:

"What does that mean—'tame'?"

"You do not live here," said the fox. "What is it that you are looking for?"

"I am looking for men," said the little prince. "What does that mean—'tame'?"

"Men," said the fox. "They have guns, and they hunt. It is very disturbing. They also raise chickens. These are their only interests. Are you looking for chickens?"

"No," said the little prince. "I am looking for friends. What does that mean—'tame'?"

"It is an act too often neglected," said the fox. "It means to establish ties."

" 'To establish ties'?"

"Just that," said the fox. "To me, you are still nothing more than a little boy who is just like a hundred thousand other little boys. And I have no need of you. And you, on your part, have no need of me. To you, I am nothing more than a fox like a hundred thousand other foxes. But if you tame me, then we shall need each other. To me, you will be unique in all the world. To you, I shall be unique in all the world . . ."

"I am beginning to understand," said the little prince. "There is a flower . . . I think that she has tamed me . . ."

"It is possible," said the fox. "On the Earth one sees all sorts of things."

"Oh, but this is not on the Earth!" said the little prince.

The fox seemed perplexed, and very curious.

"On another planet?"

"Yes."

"Are there hunters on that planet?"

"No."

"Ah, that is interesting! Are there chickens?"

"No."

"Men," said the fox. *"They have guns,
and they hunt."*

"Nothing is perfect," sighed the fox.

But he came back to his idea.

"My life is very monotonous," he said. "I hunt chickens; men hunt me. All the chickens are just alike, and all the men are just alike. And, in consequence, I am a little bored. But if you tame me, it will be as if the sun came to shine on my life. I shall know the sound of a step that will be different from all the others. Other steps send me hurrying back underneath the ground. Yours will call me, like music, out of my burrow. And then look: you see the grain-fields down yonder? I do not eat bread. Wheat is of no use to me. The wheat fields have nothing to say to me. And that is sad. But you have hair that is the color of gold. Think how wonderful that will be when you have tamed me! The grain, which is also golden, will bring me back the thought of you. And I shall love to listen to the wind in the wheat . . ."

The fox gazed at the little prince, for a long time.

"Please—tame me!" he said.

"I want to, very much," the little prince replied. "But I have not much time. I have friends to discover, and a great many things to understand."

"One only understands the things that one tames," said the fox. "Men have no more time to understand anything. They buy things all ready made at the shops. But there is no shop anywhere where one can buy friendship, and so men have no friends any more. If you want a friend, tame me . . ."

"What must I do, to tame you?" asked the little prince.

"You must be very patient," replied the fox. "First you will sit down at a little distance from me—like that—in the grass. I shall look at you out of the corner of my eye, and you will say nothing. Words are the source of misunderstandings. But you will sit a little closer to me, every day . . ."

The next day the little prince came back.

"It would have been better to come back at the same hour," said the fox. "If, for example, you come at four o'clock in the afternoon, then at three o'clock I shall begin to be happy. I shall feel happier and happier as the hour advances. At four o'clock, I shall already be worrying and jumping about. I shall show you how happy I am! But if you come at just any time, I shall never know at what hour my heart is to be ready to greet you . . . One must observe the proper rites . . ."

"What is a rite?" asked the little prince.

"Those also are actions too often neglected," said the fox. "They are what make one day different from other days, one hour from other hours. There is a rite, for example, among my hunters. Every Thursday they dance with the village girls. So Thursday is a wonderful day for me! I can take a walk as far as the vineyards. But

"If you come at four o'clock in the afternoon, then by three o'clock I shall begin to be happy."

if the hunters danced at just any time, every day would be like every other day, and I should never have any vacation at all."

So the little prince tamed the fox. And when the hour of his departure drew near—

"Ah," said the fox, "I shall cry."

"It is your own fault," said the little prince. "I never wished you any sort of harm; but you wanted me to tame you . . ."

"Yes, that is so," said the fox.

"But now you are going to cry!" said the little prince.

"Yes, that is so," said the fox.

"Then it has done you no good at all!"

"It has done me good," said the fox, "because of the color of the wheat fields." And then he added:

"Go and look again at the roses. You will understand now that yours is unique in all the world. Then come back to say goodbye to me, and I will make you a present of a secret."

The little prince went away, to look again at the roses.

"You are not at all like my rose," he said. "As yet you are nothing. No one has tamed you, and you have tamed no one. You are like my fox when I first knew him. He was only a fox like a hundred thousand other foxes. But I have made him my friend, and now he is unique in all the world."

And the roses were very much embarrassed.

"You are beautiful, but you are empty," he went on. "One could not die for you. To be sure, an ordinary passerby would think that my rose looked just like you—the rose that belongs to me. But in herself alone she is more important than all the hundreds of you other roses: because it is she that I have watered; because it is she that I have put under the glass globe; because it is she that I have sheltered behind the screen; because it is for her that I have killed the caterpillars (except the two or three that we saved to become butterflies); because it is she that I have listened to, when she grumbled, or boasted, or even sometimes when she said nothing. Because she is *my* rose."

And he went back to meet the fox.

"Goodbye," he said.

"Goodbye," said the fox. "And now here is my secret, a very simple secret: It is only with the heart that one can see rightly; what is essential is invisible to the eye."

"What is essential is invisible to the eye," the little prince repeated, so that he would be sure to remember.

"It is the time you have wasted for your rose that makes your rose so important."

"It is the time I have wasted for my rose—" said the little prince, so that he would be sure to remember.

"Men have forgotten this truth," said the fox. "But you must not forget it. You become responsible, forever, for what you have tamed. You are responsible for your rose . . ."

"I am responsible for my rose," the little prince repeated, so that he would be sure to remember.

22

"Good morning," said the little prince.

"Good morning," said the railway switchman.

"What do you do here?" the little prince asked.

"I sort out travelers, in bundles of a thousand," said the switchman. "I send off the trains that carry them: now to the right, now to the left."

And a brilliantly lighted express train shook the switchman's cabin as it rushed by with a roar like thunder.

"They are in a great hurry," said the little prince. "What are they looking for?"

"Not even the locomotive engineer knows that," said the switchman.

And a second brilliantly lighted express thundered by, in the opposite direction.

"Are they coming back already?" demanded the little prince.

"These are not the same ones," said the switch-man. "It is an exchange."

"Were they not satisfied where they were?" asked the little prince.

"No one is ever satisfied where he is," said the switchman.

And they heard the roaring thunder of a third brilliantly lighted express.

"Are they pursuing the first travelers?" demanded the little prince.

"They are pursuing nothing at all," said the switchman. "They are asleep in there, or if they are not asleep they are yawning. Only the children are flattening their noses against the windowpanes."

"Only the children know what they are looking for," said the little prince. "They waste their time over a rag doll and it becomes very important to them; and if anybody takes it away from them, they cry . . ."

"They are lucky," the switchman said.

23

"Good morning," said the little prince.

"Good morning," said the merchant.

This was a merchant who sold pills that had been invented to quench thirst. You need only swallow one pill a week, and you would feel no need of anything to drink.

"Why are you selling those?" asked the little prince.

"Because they save a tremendous amount of time," said the merchant. "Computations have been made by experts. With these pills, you save fifty-three minutes in every week."

"And what do I do with those fifty-three minutes?"

"Anything you like . . ."

"As for me," said the little prince to himself, "if I had fifty-three minutes to spend as I liked, I should walk at my leisure toward a spring of fresh water."

24

It was now the eighth day since I had had my accident in the desert, and I had listened to the story of the merchant as I was drinking the last drop of my water supply.

"Ah," I said to the little prince, "these memories of yours are very charming; but I have not yet succeeded in repairing my plane; I have nothing more to drink; and I, too, should be very happy if I could walk at my leisure toward a spring of fresh water!"

"My friend the fox—" the little prince said to me.

"My dear little man, this is no longer a matter that has anything to do with the fox!"

"Why not?"

"Because I am about to die of thirst . . ."

He did not follow my reasoning, and he answered me:

"It is a good thing to have had a friend, even if one is about to die. I, for instance, am very glad to have had a fox as a friend . . ."

"He has no way of guessing the danger," I said to myself. "He has never been either hungry or thirsty. A little sunshine is all he needs . . ."

But he looked at me steadily, and replied to my thought:

"I am thirsty, too. Let us look for a well . . ."

I made a gesture of weariness. It is absurd to look for a well, at random, in the immensity of the desert. But nevertheless we started walking.

When we had trudged along for several hours, in silence, the darkness fell, and the stars began to come out. Thirst had made me a little feverish, and I looked at them as if I were in a dream. The little prince's last words came reeling back into my memory:

"Then you are thirsty, too?" I demanded.

But he did not reply to my question. He merely said to me:

"Water may also be good for the heart . . ."

I did not understand this answer, but I said nothing. I knew very well that it was impossible to cross-examine him.

He was tired. He sat down. I sat down beside him. And, after a little silence, he spoke again:

"The stars are beautiful, because of a flower that cannot be seen."

I replied, "Yes, that is so." And, without saying anything more, I looked across the ridges of sand that were stretched out before us in the moonlight.

"The desert is beautiful," the little prince added.

And that was true. I have always loved the desert. One sits down on a desert sand dune, sees nothing, hears nothing. Yet through the silence something throbs, and gleams . . .

"What makes the desert beautiful," said the little prince, "is that somewhere it hides a well . . ."

I was astonished by a sudden understanding of that mysterious radiation of the sands. When I was a little boy I lived in an old house, and legend told us that a treasure was buried there. To be sure, no one had ever known how to find it; perhaps no one had ever even looked for it. But it cast an enchantment over that house. My home was hiding a secret in the depths of its heart . . .

"Yes," I said to the little prince. "The house, the stars, the desert—what gives them their beauty is something that is invisible!"

"I am glad," he said, "that you agree with my fox."

As the little prince dropped off to sleep, I took him in my arms and set out walking once more. I felt deeply moved, and stirred. It seemed to me that I was carrying a very fragile treasure. It seemed to me, even, that there was nothing more fragile on all the Earth. In the moonlight I looked at his pale forehead, his closed eyes, his locks of hair that trembled in the wind, and I said to myself: "What I see here is nothing but a shell. What is most important is invisible . . ."

As his lips opened slightly with the suspicion of a half-smile, I said to myself, again: "What moves me so deeply, about this little prince who is sleeping here, is his loyalty to a flower—the image of a rose that shines through his whole being like the flame of a lamp, even when he is asleep . . ." And I felt him to be more fragile still. I felt the need of protecting him, as if he himself were a flame that might be extinguished by a little puff of wind . . .

And, as I walked on so, I found the well, at daybreak.

25

"Men," said the little prince, "set out on their way in express trains, but they do not know what they are looking for. Then they rush about, and get excited, and turn round and round . . ."

And he added:

"It is not worth the trouble . . ."

The well that we had come to was not like the wells of the Sahara. The wells of the Sahara are mere holes dug in the sand. This one was like a well in a village. But there was no village here, and I thought I must be dreaming . . .

"It is strange," I said to the little prince. "Everything is ready for use: the pulley, the bucket, the rope . . ."

He laughed, touched the rope, and set the pulley to working. And the pulley moaned, like an old weathervane which the wind has long since forgotten.

"He laughed, touched the rope, and set the pulley to working."

"Do you hear?" said the little prince. "We have wakened the well, and it is singing . . ."

I did not want him to tire himself with the rope.

"Leave it to me," I said. "It is too heavy for you."

I hoisted the bucket slowly to the edge of the well and set it there—happy, tired as I was, over my achievement. The song of the pulley was still in my ears, and I could see the sunlight shimmer in the still trembling water.

"I am thirsty for this water," said the little prince. "Give me some of it to drink . . ."

And I understood what he had been looking for.

I raised the bucket to his lips. He drank, his eyes closed. It was as sweet as some special festival treat. This water was indeed a different thing from ordinary nourishment. Its sweetness was born of the walk under the stars, the song of the pulley, the effort of my arms. It was good for the heart, like a present. When I was a little boy, the lights of the Christmas tree, the music of the Midnight Mass, the tenderness of smiling faces, used to make up, so, the radiance of the gifts I received.

"The men where you live," said the little prince, "raise five thousand roses in the same garden—and they do not find in it what they are looking for."

"They do not find it," I replied.

"And yet what they are looking for could be found in one single rose, or in a little water."

"Yes, that is true," I said.

And the little prince added:

"But the eyes are blind. One must look with the heart . . ."

I had drunk the water. I breathed easily. At sunrise the sand is the color of honey. And that honey color was making me happy, too. What brought me, then, this sense of grief?

"You must keep your promise," said the little prince, softly, as he sat down beside me once more.

"What promise?"

"You know—a muzzle for my sheep . . . I am responsible for this flower . . ."

I took my rough drafts of drawings out of my pocket. The little prince looked them over, and laughed as he said:

"Your baobabs—they look a little like cabbages."

"Oh!"

I had been so proud of my baobabs!

"Your fox—his ears look a little like horns; and they are too long."

And he laughed again.

"You are not fair, little prince," I said. "I don't know how to draw anything except boa constrictors from the outside and boa constrictors from the inside."

"Oh, that will be all right," he said, "children understand."

So then I made a pencil sketch of a muzzle. And as I gave it to him my heart was torn.

"You have plans that I do not know about," I said.

But he did not answer me. He said to me, instead:

"You know—my descent to the earth . . . Tomorrow will be its anniversary."

Then, after a silence, he went on:

"I came down very near here."

And he flushed.

And once again, without understanding why, I had a queer sense of sorrow. One question, however, occurred to me:

"Then it was not by chance that on the morning when I first met you—a week ago—you were strolling along like that, all alone, a thousand miles from any inhabited region? You were on your way back to the place where you landed?"

The little prince flushed again.

And I added, with some hesitancy:

"Perhaps it was because of the anniversary?"

The little prince flushed once more. He never answered questions—but when one flushes does that not mean "Yes"?

"Ah," I said to him, "I am a little frightened—"

But he interrupted me.

"Now you must work. You must return to your engine. I will be waiting for you here. Come back tomorrow evening . . ."

But I was not reassured. I remembered the fox. One runs the risk of weeping a little, if one lets himself be tamed . . .

26

Beside the well there was the ruin of an old stone wall. When I came back from my work, the next evening, I saw from some distance away my little prince sitting on top of this wall, with his feet dangling. And I heard him say:

"Then you don't remember. This is not the exact spot."

Another voice must have answered him, for he replied to it:

"Yes, yes! It is the right day, but this is not the place."

I continued my walk toward the wall. At no time did I see or hear anyone. The little prince, however, replied once again:

"—Exactly. You will see where my track begins, in the sand. You have nothing to do but wait for me there. I shall be there tonight."

I was only twenty meters from the wall, and I still saw nothing.

After a silence the little prince spoke again:

"You have good poison? You are sure that it will not make me suffer too long?"

I stopped in my tracks, my heart torn asunder; but still I did not understand.

"Now go away," said the little prince. "I want to get down from the wall."

I dropped my eyes, then, to the foot of the wall —and I leaped into the air. There before me, facing the little prince, was one of those yellow snakes that take just thirty seconds to bring your life to an end. Even as I was digging into my pocket to get out my revolver I made a running step back. But, at the noise I made, the snake let himself flow easily across the sand like the dying spray of a fountain, and, in no apparent hurry, disappeared, with a light metallic sound, among the stones.

I reached the wall just in time to catch my little man in my arms; his face was white as snow.

"What does this mean?" I demanded. "Why are you talking with snakes?"

I had loosened the golden muffler that he always wore. I had moistened his temples, and had given him some water to drink. And now I did not dare ask him any more questions. He looked at me very gravely, and put his arms around my neck. I felt his heart beating like the heart of a dying bird, shot with someone's rifle . . .

"I am glad that you have found what was the matter with your engine," he said. "Now you can go back home—"

*"Now go away . . . I want to get down
from the wall."*

"How do you know about that?"

I was just coming to tell him that my work had been successful, beyond anything that I had dared to hope.

He made no answer to my question, but he added:

"I, too, am going back home today . . ."

Then, sadly—

"It is much farther . . . It is much more difficult . . ."

I realized clearly that something extraordinary was happening. I was holding him close in my arms as if he were a little child; and yet it seemed to me that he was rushing headlong toward an abyss from which I could do nothing to restrain him . . .

His look was very serious, like some one lost far away.

"I have your sheep. And I have the sheep's box. And I have the muzzle . . ."

And he gave me a sad smile.

I waited a long time. I could see that he was reviving little by little.

"Dear little man," I said to him, "you are afraid . . ."

He was afraid, there was no doubt about that. But he laughed lightly.

"I shall be much more afraid this evening . . ."

Once again I felt myself frozen by the sense of

something irreparable. And I knew that I could not bear the thought of never hearing that laughter any more. For me, it was like a spring of fresh water in the desert.

"Little man," I said, "I want to hear you laugh again."

But he said to me:

"Tonight, it will be a year . . . My star, then, can be found right above the place where I came to the Earth, a year ago . . ."

"Little man," I said, "tell me that it is only a bad dream—this affair of the snake, and the meeting-place, and the star . . ."

But he did not answer my plea. He said to me, instead:

"The thing that is important is the thing that is not seen . . ."

"Yes, I know . . ."

"It is just as it is with the flower. If you love a flower that lives on a star, it is sweet to look at the sky at night. All the stars are a-bloom with flowers . . ."

"Yes, I know . . ."

"It is just as it is with the water. Because of the pulley, and the rope, what you gave me to drink was like music. You remember—how good it was."

"Yes, I know . . ."

"And at night you will look up at the stars. Where I live everything is so small that I cannot show you where my star is to be found. It is better, like that. My star will just be one of the stars, for you. And so you will love to watch all the stars in the heavens . . . They will all be your friends. And, besides, I am going to make you a present . . ."

He laughed again.

"Ah, little prince, dear little prince! I love to hear that laughter!"

"That is my present. Just that. It will be as it was when we drank the water . . ."

"What are you trying to say?"

"All men have the stars," he answered, "but they are not the same things for different people. For some, who are travelers, the stars are guides. For others they are no more than little lights in the sky. For others, who are scholars, they are problems. For my businessman they were wealth. But all these stars are silent. You—you alone— will have the stars as no one else has them—"

"What are you trying to say?"

"In one of the stars I shall be living. In one of them I shall be laughing. And so it will be as if all the stars were laughing, when you look at the sky at night . . . You—only you—will have stars that can laugh!"

And he laughed again.

"And when your sorrow is comforted (time soothes all sorrows) you will be content that you have known me. You will always be my friend. You will want to laugh with me. And you will sometimes open your window, so, for that pleasure . . . And your friends will be properly astonished to see you laughing as you look up at the sky! Then you will say to them, 'Yes, the stars always make me laugh!' And they will think you are crazy. It will be a very shabby trick that I shall have played on you . . ."

And he laughed again.

"It will be as if, in place of the stars, I had given you a great number of little bells that knew how to laugh . . ."

And he laughed again. Then he quickly became serious:

"Tonight—you know . . . Do not come."

"I shall not leave you," I said.

"I shall look as if I were suffering. I shall look a little as if I were dying. It is like that. Do not come to see that. It is not worth the trouble . . ."

"I shall not leave you."

But he was worried.

"I tell you—it is also because of the snake. He must not bite you. Snakes—they are malicious creatures. This one might bite you just for fun . . ."

"I shall not leave you."

But a thought came to reassure him:

"It is true that they have no more poison for a second bite."

That night I did not see him set out on his way. He got away from me without making a sound. When I succeeded in catching up with him he was walking along with a quick and resolute step. He said to me merely:

"Ah! You are there . . ."

And he took me by the hand. But he was still worrying.

"It was wrong of you to come. You will suffer. I shall look as if I were dead; and that will not be true . . ."

I said nothing.

"You understand . . . It is too far. I cannot carry this body with me. It is too heavy."

I said nothing.

"But it will be like an old abandoned shell. There is nothing sad about old shells . . ."

I said nothing.

He was a little discouraged. But he made one more effort:

"You know, it will be very nice. I, too, shall look at the stars. All the stars will be wells with a rusty pulley. All the stars will pour out fresh water for me to drink . . ."

I said nothing.

"That will be so amusing! You will have five hundred million little bells, and I shall have five hundred million springs of fresh water . . ."

And he too said nothing more, because he was crying . . .

"Here it is. Let me go on by myself."

And he sat down, because he was afraid. Then he said, again:

"You know—my flower . . . I am responsible for her. And she is so weak! She is so naïve! She has four thorns, of no use at all, to protect herself against all the world . . ."

I too sat down, because I was not able to stand up any longer.

"There now—that is all . . ."

He still hesitated a little; then he got up. He took one step. I could not move.

There was nothing there but a flash of yellow close to his ankle. He remained motionless for an instant. He did not cry out. He fell as gently as a tree falls. There was not even any sound, because of the sand.

27

And now six years have already gone by . . .
I have never yet told this story. The companions
who met me on my return were well content to
see me alive. I was sad, but I told them: "I am
tired."

Now my sorrow is comforted a little. That is
to say—not entirely. But I know that he did go
back to his planet, because I did not find his body
at daybreak. It was not such a heavy body . . .
And at night I love to listen to the stars. It is like
five hundred million little bells . . .

But there is one extraordinary thing . . .
When I drew the muzzle for the little prince, I forgot to add the leather strap to it. He will never
have been able to fasten it on his sheep. So now I
keep wondering: what is happening on his planet?
Perhaps the sheep has eaten the flower . . .

At one time I say to myself: "Surely not! The
little prince shuts his flower under her glass globe
every night, and he watches over his sheep very
carefully . . ." Then I am happy. And there is
sweetness in the laughter of all the stars.

But at another time I say to myself: "At some
moment or other one is absent-minded, and
that is enough! On some one evening he forgot the

"He fell as gently as a tree falls. There was not even any sound . . ."

glass globe, or the sheep got out, without making any noise, in the night . . ." And then the little bells are changed to tears . . .

Here, then, is a great mystery. For you who also love the little prince, and for me, nothing in the universe can be the same if somewhere, we do not know where, a sheep that we never saw has—yes or no?—eaten a rose . . .

Look up at the sky. Ask yourselves: Is it yes or no? Has the sheep eaten the flower? And you will see how everything changes . . .

And no grown-up will ever understand that this is a matter of so much importance!

This is, to me, the loveliest and saddest landscape in the world. It is the same as that on the preceding page, but I have drawn it again to impress it on your memory. It is here that the little prince appeared on Earth, and disappeared.

Look at it carefully so that you will be sure to recognize it in case you travel some day to the African desert. And, if you should come upon this spot, please do not hurry on. Wait for a time, exactly under the star. Then, if a little man appears who laughs, who has golden hair and who refuses to answer questions, you will know who he is. If this should happen, please comfort me. Send me word that he has come back.

Books by
ANTOINE DE SAINT EXUPÉRY
available in paperbound editions from
Harcourt Brace Jovanovich, Inc.

FLIGHT TO ARRAS
DER KLEINE PRINZ
THE LITTLE PRINCE
NIGHT FLIGHT
LE PETIT PRINCE
EL PRINCIPITO
SOUTHERN MAIL
WIND, SAND AND STARS

W9-CGK-144

Do you sometimes think God does not hear? That your cries of pain fade into nothing?

God is not deaf. He is as grieved by the world's trauma as you are. His only Son died here. But He has promised to set things right. Nothing simply disappears.

Let history finish. Let the symphony scratch out its last mournful note of discord before it bursts into song. As Paul said, "In my opinion whatever we may have to go through now is less than nothing compared with the magnificent future God has planned for us. . . . It is plain to anyone with eyes to see that at the present time all created life groans in a sort of universal travail. And it is plain, too, that we who have a foretaste of the Spirit are in a state of painful tension, while we wait for that redemption of our bodies which will mean that at last we have realized our full sonship in him."

—from WHERE IS GOD WHEN IT HURTS?

Also by Philip Yancey

Disappointment With God

Published by
HARPERPAPERBACKS

ATTENTION: ORGANIZATIONS AND CORPORATIONS

Most HarperPaperbacks are available at special quantity discounts for bulk purchases for sales promotions, premiums, or fund-raising. For information, please call or write:
Special Markets Department, HarperCollins Publishers,
10 East 53rd Street, New York, N.Y. 10022.
Telephone: (212) 207-7528. Fax: (212) 207-7222.

PHILIP YANCEY

WHERE IS GOD WHEN IT HURTS?

HarperPaperbacks

A Division of HarperCollinsPublishers

If you purchased this book without a cover, you should be
aware that this book is stolen property. It was reported as
"unsold and destroyed" to the publisher and neither the
author nor the publisher has received any payment for this
"stripped book."

HarperPaperbacks   *A Division of* HarperCollins*Publishers*
                    10 East 53rd Street, New York, N.Y. 10022

Copyright © 1977 by The Zondervan Corporation
All rights reserved. No part of this book may be used or
reproduced in any manner whatsoever without written
permission of the publisher, except in the case of brief
quotations embodied in critical articles and reviews. For
information address Zondervan Publishing House,
1415 Lake Drive, S.E., Grand Rapids, MI 49506

This book was published by arrangement with Zondervan
Publishing House.

First HarperPaperbacks printing: November 1990

Printed in the United States of America

HarperPaperbacks and colophon are trademarks of
HarperCollins*Publishers*

10 9 8

To Dr. Paul Brand, who
unselfishly shared with me
a lifetime of medical
and spiritual wisdom.

Contents

Think too
   of all who suffer
      as if
         you
            shared their pain.

Hebrews 13:3 J.B. PHILLIPS

*Meanwhile, where is God? This is one of the most
disquieting symptoms. When you are happy, so happy that
you have no sense of needing Him, if you turn to Him then
with praise, you will be welcomed with open arms. But go
to Him when your need is desperate, when all other help is
vain and what do you find? A door slammed in your face,
and a sound of bolting and double bolting on the inside.
After that, silence. You may as well turn away.*

C. S. Lewis
A Grief Observed

* 1 *

A Problem That Won't Go Away

I feel helpless around people in great pain. Really, I feel guilty. They lie alone, perhaps moaning, their features twitching, and there is no way I can span the gulf between us to penetrate their suffering. I can only watch. Anything I attempt to say seems weak and stiff, as if I'd memorized the lines for a school play.

Several years ago, I heard a frantic call for help from close friends, John and Claudia Claxton. They were newlyweds, in their early twenties, beginning life together in the Midwest. I had never seen love affect anyone as thoroughly as it had affected John Claxton. In two years of engagement to Claudia he had changed from a cold, hard cynic into an optimist intent on enjoying the adventure of marriage.

The letter I received from John troubled me as soon as I opened it. Errors and scratches marred his usually neat handwriting. He explained, "Excuse my writing... I guess it shows how I'm fumbling for words. I don't know what to say." The Claxtons' young marriage had run into a roadblock far bigger than both of them. Claudia had contracted Hodgkin's disease, cancer of the lymph glands, and had been given only a 50 percent chance to live.

Within a week surgeons had cut her from armpit to belly and removed every visible trace of the disease. She was left stunned and weak, lying in a hospital bed.

At the time, John was working as a chaplain's assistant in a local hospital. His compassion for other patients dipped dangerously. "In some ways," he told me, "I could understand better what other patients were undergoing. But I didn't care any more; I only cared about Claudia. I wanted to scream at them, 'Stop that sniveling, you idiots! You think you've got problems— my wife may be dying right now!'"

Though both John and Claudia were strong Christians, anger against God surged up—anger against a partner they loved who had turned on them. "God, why us?" they cried. "Have You teasingly doled out some scant year of marriage to set us up for this?"

Cobalt treatments caused Claudia's body to deteriorate. Beauty fled her. She was constantly tired, her skin turned dark, her hair fell out, and her throat was always swollen and raw. She regurgitated nearly everything she ate. For a time doctors suspended treatment because her throat had become so swollen she couldn't swallow.

Each day Claudia would think about God and about her suffering, especially in the treatment room. In that chill steel room she would be laid out flat on a table, naked, where she would listen to the whir and click of machinery bombarding her with invisible particles. Each day of the radiation aged her body by months.

_____ **Claudia's Visitors** _____

At first Claudia had expected that Christian visitors would console and comfort her. But their voices were too confusing.

A deacon from her church solemnly told her to reflect on what God was trying to teach her. "Surely there's something in your life which is displeasing to God," he said. "You must have stepped out of His will somewhere. These things don't just *happen*. What is God telling you?"

A lady came, a scatterbrained, plump widow who saw her calling as a professional cheerleader to the sick. She brought flowers, sang hymns, and quoted happy psalms about running brooks and mountains clapping their hands. Whenever Claudia's illness was mentioned, this lady quickly changed the subject. Her approach was to drive out the suffering with her cheer and good will. But after she left, the flowers faded, the hymns seemed dissonant and muted, and Claudia remained to face another day of pain.

Another lady dropped by who had faithfully watched Oral Roberts, Kathryn Kuhlman, and "The 700 Club" over the years. She told Claudia that healing was the only escape. "Sickness is never God's will," she insisted. "The Bible says as much. The devil is at work, and God will wait until you can muster up enough faith to believe that you'll be healed. Remember, Claudia, faith can move mountains, and that includes Hodgkin's disease. Truly believe that you'll be healed, and God will answer your prayers."

The next few mornings, as Claudia lay in the sterile cobalt treatment room, she tried to "muster up" faith. She had faith enough to believe God was able to heal her. But she didn't know how to convince God that her faith was genuine and strong. Faith wasn't like a muscle, which she could enlarge through exercise. It was slippery, theoretical, hard to deal with. The whole notion of mustering up faith seemed awfully exhausting to her, and she could never decide how to go about it.

Perhaps the most spiritual lady in Claudia's church came to read aloud books about praising God for everything. "Claudia, you need to come to the place where you can say, 'God, I *love* You for making me suffer like this. It is Your will. You know the best for me. And I just praise You for loving me enough to allow me to experience this. In all things, including this, I give thanks.'"

As she pondered the words, Claudia's mind filled with ferocious, gruesome visions of God. She imagined a figure in the shape of a troll, big as the universe, who delighted in squeezing helpless humans between his fingernails, pulverizing them with his fists, dashing them against sharp stones. The figure would keep torturing these humans until they cried out, "God, I love You for doing this to me!" The idea repulsed Claudia. She could not worship or love such a God.

Yet another visitor, Claudia's pastor, made her feel she was on a select mission. He told her, "You, Claudia, can participate in Christ's sufferings. You have been appointed to suffer for Him, and He will reward you. God chose you because of your great strength and integrity, just as He chose Job. And He is using you as an example. The faith of others may increase because of your response."

Sometimes, in a self-pitying sort of way, the thought of being a privileged martyr appealed to Claudia. Other times, when the aches crescendoed, when food was painfully vomited up, and when her facial features aged, Claudia would call out, "God, why me? There are millions of Christians stronger and more honorable than I—couldn't you choose one of them?"

_____ **The Great Defect** _____

I, too, visited Claudia during her illness. She repeated for me the parcels of advice which well-meaning Christians had left her. I listened to her bewildered response. She didn't know what kind of lesson she was supposed to be learning. Nor did she know how to have more faith. But she was sure of one thing: her happy world with John was disintegrating and, above all, she didn't want it to end.

Why was Claudia moaning in a hospital bed while I stood beside her, healthy? What new words of Christian advice could I add? Something inside me recoiled as I heard the clichéd comments to sufferers floating through the hospital corridors. Is Christianity supposed to confuse the sufferer or, rather, help him?

And so, because of questions which arose from my

contacts with Claudia* and others like her, I began a
quest which has lasted for several years and culminates
in this book. I have looked for a message we Christians
can give to those who are suffering. And, I've hunted a
message which can strengthen my own faith if I suffer.
Where is God when it hurts? Is He trying to tell us
something?

After an extensive tour of the United States, the well-
known German pastor and theologian Helmut Thielicke
was asked what he saw as the greatest defect among
American Christians. He replied, "They have an inadequate view of suffering." I have come to agree with him.

The defect stands out as a huge blemish to the non-
Christian world. I've asked college students what they
have against Christianity, and most of them echo var-
iations on the theme of suffering. "I can't believe in a
God who would allow Auschwitz and Northern Ireland";
"My teen-age sister died of leukemia despite all the
Christians' prayers"; "One-third of the world went to
bed hungry last night—how does that square with
Christian love?"

As I read books on pain, I discovered that many great
philosophers, otherwise sympathetic to Christian principles and ethics, have stumbled at this problem of pain
and suffering, ultimately rejecting Christianity because
of it. C. E. M. Joad wrote, "What, then, are the arguments
which for me have told so strongly against the religious
view of the universe? ... First, there was the difficulty

*Claudia's dilemma eventually was resolved when the cobalt treat-
ments effectively destroyed the cancer cells. Five years have passed,
and she's had no recurrence of the disease.

presented by the facts of pain and evil."[1] Other philosophers, such as Bertrand Russell and Voltaire, eloquently share Joad's complaint.

The messy problem of pain and suffering keeps popping up, regardless of our erudite attempts to explain it away. Even C. S. Lewis, who offered perhaps the most articulate explanation of it in this century, saw his arguments fade in significance as he watched the onslaught of bone cancer in his wife's body. "You never know how much you really believe anything until its truth or falsehood becomes a matter of life and death to you," he said.

Like Hercules' battle against the Hydra, all our attempts to chop down agnostic arguments are met with writhing new examples of suffering. And our Christian defense usually sounds like a red-faced, foot-shuffling, lowered-head apology.

_____ **A Personal Approach** _____

I will not attempt to address philosophers with this book. Others with far more training have done that. Rather, I have tried to keep before me the scene of my friend, Claudia Claxton, lying on a hospital bed. Most of our problems with pain are not mental gymnastics. They are Claudia's problems: a raw throat, the specter of a new marriage gouged by death, a loss of youth, the paralyzing fear of the unknown.

To prepare for this book, I talked to Christians who suffer at a level far worse than most of us will ever experience. For some of them, pain is their life. It is the first sensation to greet them in the morning and the last they feel before drifting off to sleep, if they are lucky enough to fall asleep despite it. You will meet these people in depth later in the book.

Ironically, I also spent time among people with leprosy, people who cannot suffer in the physiological sense but desperately wish they could.

Perhaps the next time I'm sick, when the flu hits and I toss in bed, fighting off waves of nausea—perhaps then my conclusions about pain will be of no solace. But as a Christian trying to fathom what God is up to in this world, I have learned a great deal. My anger and bitterness against God have subsided as I've come to realize why He allows this bleeding world.

Some large philosophical questions I will leave almost untouched. In what form did evil enter the world? Why is suffering distributed so inequitably? Why natural disasters? Instead, I will enter the world of the sufferer to find out what difference it makes to be a Christian there.

First, I will examine pain through the microscope, biologically, to see what role it plays in life. Then, stepping back, I will look at our planet as a whole, asking what God is up to. Is suffering God's one great goof?

At that point, I will visit in detail several extraordinary, fascinating people to ask their response to pain. And, finally, I will ask myself what response I can give as I suffer and as I reach out to others.

PART 1

✳

Why Is There Such a Thing As Pain?

Thank God for inventing pain. I don't think He could have done a better job.

Dr. Paul Brand

* 2 *
The Gift
Nobody Wants

I am sitting in Chicago's ornate Orchestra Hall. I have exulted in the Beethoven and Mozart pieces, but the long, complicated Prokofiev concerto is another matter. Energy-giving blood drains toward my stomach to digest the Sunday brunch, and I find it increasingly difficult to stay awake.

Gradually the music fuses together into one faint, distant tone, and my eyelids sag. I look around me and see scores of well-dressed concertgoers who have already succumbed. And so I rest my chin on my right hand and prop my elbow on the wooden armrest. The music fades....

THUNK!! My limbs are splayed out in all directions. People in the seats around me are glaring, their necks craned in my direction. My overcoat is on the floor. Startled and embarrassed, I retrieve the overcoat, straighten in my seat, and try to concentrate on the music. Blood is pounding in my head.

What happened? While I was drifting into dreamland, my body was working to protect me. As my head nodded lower, my arms suddenly jerked out in a spasm, my head shot upward, and my whole torso twitched. Though an embarrassment to me, the activity was merely the body's loyal effort to prevent my injury. Two small sacs in my inner ear, filled with fluid and lined with ultra-sensitive hairs, had detected an alarming shift in my equilibrium. Just at the last moment, as my head was about to crash downward to the armrest, the inner ear sounded an all-points-alert. With remarkable speed all my limbs responded dramatically, and I was saved from injury. All these complex maneuvers had taken place while I was drifting off to sleep.

_____ Danger Detector _____

Pain sensors normally operate precisely like these sensors in the inner ear. They warn my body of impending (or present) danger. The feeling of pain forces my body to concentrate on a problem area and respond to it. Sometimes the reaction is almost subconscious. For example, when I go to the doctor for a checkup and he taps my knee with a rubber hammer, my leg straightens violently. The automatic reaction occurs because the doctor's stimulus gives the knee the impression that it is bending. His hammer hits the same nerves that would be affected if my knee would suddenly buckle while walking. My body rushes to compensate, lest I stumble and experience a greater pain. The reaction is too spontaneous and lightning-quick to allow the brain time to reason that I'm seated on a table, not standing, and there is really no danger of falling.

Despite their protective value, the nervous system and its millions of pain sensors are the most unappreciated bodily functions. They attract mostly abuse and bad feelings.

I have never read a poem extolling the virtues of pain, nor seen a statue erected in its honor, nor heard a hymn dedicated to it. Pain is usually defined as "unpleasantness."

Christians don't really know how to interpret pain. If you pinned them against the wall, in a dark, secret moment, many Christians would probably admit that pain was God's one mistake. He really should have worked a little harder and invented a better way of coping with the world's dangers.

I am convinced that pain gets a bad press. Perhaps we should see statues, hymns, and poems to pain. Why do I think that? Because up close, under a microscope, the pain network is seen in an entirely different light. It is perhaps the paragon of creative genius.

My discussion of pain, then, must begin by examining the human body. Why does my body need pain? When I hurt, what is it telling me? I must start here with the close-up view before I can look into the faces of suffering people.

(Of necessity, this discussion will be more technical and biological than the rest of the book. It builds a framework from which I can later address more personal viewpoints.

If biology is not your forte and you generally skip TV specials on "The incredible human body," you may want to skim this chapter. I begin here because the microscopic view is the one most often overlooked by people fumbling with the question "Where is God when it hurts?")

_____ **Trying to Re-invent Pain** _____

I was most impressed with the amazing effectiveness of the pain network when I visited Dr. Paul Brand* of Carville, Louisiana, the only man I've met who crusades on behalf of pain. Without hesitation, Dr. Brand announces, "Thank God for inventing pain! I don't think He could have done a better job. It's beautiful." Dr. Brand is well-qualified to make such a judgment, since he is one of the world's foremost experts on leprosy, which attacks the nervous system.

Dr. Brand's appreciation for pain climaxed after he was given a substantial grant to design an artificial pain system. He hoped to help people with diseases that destroyed pain sensors. Brand had to try to think like the Creator, anticipating the needs of the body. After signing on three professors of electronic engineering, a bioengineer, and several research biochemists, he began.

First, the team developed an artificial nerve which could be placed on the fingertip like a glove. The nerve responded to pressure with an electric current which stimulated a warning signal.

---

*Dr. Brand has received the prestigious Albert Lasker medical award and was named Commander of the British Empire by Queen Elizabeth. His biography is *Ten Fingers for God* by Dorothy Clarke Wilson.

For five years Dr. Brand and his assistants tackled the technical problems. The more they studied nerves, the more complex their task appeared. At what level should the sensor sound a warning? How could a sensor distinguish between the normal pressure of gripping a railing and the pressure of gripping a thornbush? How could they allow for tough activities such as tennis-playing and yet warn of danger?

Brand also noticed that nerve cells change their perception of pain to meet the body's needs. When inflamed with an infection, a fingertip may become ten times as sensitive to pain as normal. That's why a swollen finger feels awkward and in the way. Nerve cells "turn up the volume," magnifying bumps and scrapes that are usually ignored. In no way could these well-funded scientists duplicate that feat with current technology.

All the artificial sensors proved fragile and would rupture or deteriorate from metal fatigue or corrosion after a few hundred uses. Each month Dr. Brand and his colleagues gained more appreciation for the remarkable engineering of the body's pain network.

_____ **Tough, Tender Skin** _____

A close look at the human body shows the incredible challenge Dr. Brand's team had chosen. They were concerned only with the surface area of the body, the skin, a flexible/tough organ which stretches over the body's frame as an advance guard against the world.

The skin is blessed with millions of pain sensors spread across its surface. Yet they aren't scattered randomly; they are distributed precisely to the areas which need them most.

Scientists have developed techniques for measuring

just how much pressure is needed for a blindfolded person to be aware of an object he's encountering. The scale, called the *absolute threshold of touch*, is measured in grams (per square millimeter of skin surface). The tip of my tongue can sense just 2 grams of applied pressure. Fingers are also incredibly sensitive—they can detect a pressure of just 3 grams. But less critical areas of skin do not need such sensitivity. The back of my hand first notices a pressure of 12 grams, and the back of my forearm is first triggered by a pressure of 33 grams. The sole of my foot, which faces a daily rigor of stomping, squeezing, and supporting weight, will only detect pressure which exceeds 250 grams![1]

Thus, while the most discerning parts of the body, such as fingers and tongue, can detect a feather touch, others need a good sound slap before they report unusual activity to the brain.

There's another test which measures the *absolute threshold of pain*. In this test, the scientist measures *how much pressure must be applied to a very sharp needle* before the subject begins to experience pain. Note how these figures contrast with the thresholds of pressure.[2]

Cornea	10.2	grams will produce painful sensations
Forearm	20	grams will produce painful sensations
Back of hand	100	grams will produce painful sensations
Sole of foot	200	grams will produce painful sensations
Fingertip	300	grams will produce painful sensations

There is an astounding difference in the fingertip. I can notice a mere 3 grams of pressure on my fingertips. But that pressure must be 300 grams before I feel pain there! Why? Think about the finger's activities. The concert violinist must feel an amazing range of pressures to produce perfect sound and volume. A baker, swishing his hands through batches of dough, can actually sense slight variations in water content—a skilled baker can notice even a 2 percent variance in the "stickiness" or consistency. Cloth feelers in textile industries compare the qualities of cloth by touch. So the fingertips need to be incredibly sensitive to the slightest differences in touch.*

But that's not enough. The fingertips must also be tough to withstand rigorous activity. Feel the calloused, scaly hand of a carpenter or a professional tennis player. Life would be miserable if the fingertip shot a message of pain to the brain every time a person squeezed a tennis racket or pounded a hammer. So the design of the body includes a fingertip extraordinarily sensitive to pressure, but relatively insensitive to pain. Our hands and fingertips serve us well as the most used parts of the body.**

---

*Though its sensors are impressively sensitive, the skin is crudely primitive compared to the sensitivity of eye and ear sensors, which detect changes in light and vibration. It takes 100 million to 10,000 million times as much energy to produce a touch sensation as to produce a hearing or visual sensation.

**Scientists measure another phenomenon of the nervous system called the *two-point threshold*. Pain cells, though innumerable, are not spread across the body capriciously. We have exactly as many as we need. The two-point test measures skin sensitivity by pressing two pins or two bristles against the skin of a blindfolded person to see how close together they must be brought before that person feels *one* pinprick rather than two. In other words, it demonstrates how close together the individual pain sensors are. On the leg, I can no longer distinguish two pinpricks when the pins are brought in to a distance of 68 mm. But I can distinguish two pinpricks on the back of the hand at a distance of 32 mm, and on the fingertip at only 2

The cornea of the eye, however, lives a different life. Having transparent surroundings, it is very fragile and has a limited blood supply. A small wound can produce blindness, and any intrusion in the eye, such as a wood splinter or a speck of dirt, is a serious problem to be reckoned with. Therefore the cornea's pain sensors have an electronic hot line to the brain so responsive that a stray eyelash will cause instant irritation.

_____ Colic, Kidney Stones, and Heart Attacks _____

Dr. Brand's team ran into insurmountable difficulties designing an artificial pain network just for the skin. Inside the body is an even more perplexing situation. Measurements for the skin are made with such tests as pinpricks and heat burns. Those tests would not work on internal organs, which feature unique sets of pain receptors. The skin absorbs the shock of cuts and burns and pressures, so internal organs can get along without such elaborate warning systems. Once past the skin, you could burn the stomach with a match or cut the brain with a knife or crush the kidney, and a patient would feel no pain. Why? Those pain defenses aren't needed. Internal organs are seldom exposed to such danger—the skin and skeleton protect them.

Yet if a doctor inserts a balloon inside my stomach and fills it with air to distend my stomach slightly, pain signals would shoot to my brain—the pain of colic, or

mm apart. On the tip of the tongue, however, the distance is only 1 mm. This explains the common phenomenon I feel when food is caught in between my teeth. With my tongue I can search it out and quickly determine in what crack the food is caught. But with the fingertip, the food is harder to locate. Spaces between the teeth "feel smaller" with the finger than with the tongue.[3]

gas pains. The stomach's pain network is designed to respond to its specific dangers. Likewise, the kidney sends out excruciating pain signals when a BB-sized kidney stone is present.

If an internal organ must inform the brain of an emergency danger its pain sensors are not designed to handle, the organ uses the remarkable phenomenon of *referred pain*. It "borrows" nearby pain sensors to alert the body to danger. For example, heart attack victims may notice a tenderness in skin on the left side of the chest. The skin is not in danger; it is merely borrowed by the heart as a relay warning station. Similarly, appendicitis can be difficult to diagnose because the appendix may borrow pain sensors in a variety of places, such as either side near the kidneys.

Such facts as these—the exact distribution of needed pain cells, the pressure/pain thresholds, and the backup system of referred pain convince me that *whatever it is, the pain network is not an accident*.

It is not God's great goof or an afterthought. Rather, it is indelibly stamped with a marvelous design. It fits our bodies well. Pain is as essential to a normal functioning life, it could be argued, as eyesight or even good circulation. Without pain, as we shall see, our lives would be fraught with danger, and we would do without such basic pleasures as sports and hobbies.

_____ **But Must It Hurt?** _____
Almost everyone who studies the body will admit that the nervous system is well-engineered. But one could naturally ask, "Does pain have to be unpleasant? A protective system is, of course, necessary, but must it *hurt?* What about when a piercing shot of pain races to the

brain, doubling up a patient—couldn't God have found another way of alerting us?"

Dr. Brand's team contemplated these questions as they worked on an artificial nerve cell. For a long time they used an audible signal coming through a hearing aid, a signal that would hum when the tissues were receiving normal pressures and buzz loudly when the tissues were actually in danger. But the signal was not unpleasant enough. A patient would tolerate a loud noise if he wanted to do something such as turn a screwdriver too hard, even though the signal told him it could be harmful. Blinking lights were tried and eliminated for the same reason. Brand finally resorted to electric shock to make people let go of something that might hurt them. People had to be *forced* to remove their hands; being alerted to the danger was insufficient. The stimulus had to be unpleasant, just as pain is unpleasant.

"We also found out that the signal had to be out of the patient's reach," Brand says. "For even intelligent people, if they wished to do something which they were afraid would activate the shock, would switch off the signal, do what they had in mind to do, and then switch it on again when there was no danger of receiving an unpleasant signal. I remember thinking how wise God had been in putting pain out of reach."

After five years of work, thousands of man-hours, and over a million dollars, Dr. Brand and his associates abandoned the entire project. A warning system suitable for just one hand was exorbitantly expensive, subject to frequent mechanical breakdown, and hopelessly inadequate to interpret the mass of sensations the hand encounters. The system sometimes called "God's great mistake" was far too complex for even the most sophisticated technology to mimic.

Paul Brand says with utter sincerity, "Thank God for pain!" By definition, pain is unpleasant, enough so to force us to withdraw our fingers from a stove. Yet, that very quality saves us from destruction. Unless the warning signal *demands* response, we might not heed it.

For someone with crippling arthritis or terminal cancer, pain rages out of control, and any relief, especially a painless world, would seem like heaven itself. But for the majority of us, the pain network performs daily protective service. It is effectively designed for surviving life on this sometimes hostile planet.

Pain, then, is not God's great goof. It is a gift—the gift that nobody wants. Without it, our lives would be open to abuse and horrible decay.

More than anything, pain should be viewed as a communication network. It unites our body, simultaneously guarding our various parts and knitting them together for the common goal of protecting us.

I do not say that all pain is good. Sometimes it flares up and makes life miserable—but even then it is usually giving intense warning signals about a serious disease. And the idea of the "gift of pain" does not speak to many of the problems connected with suffering. But it is a beginning point of a realistic perspective on pain and suffering.

Too often the emotional trauma of intense pain blinds us to its inherent value. When I break an arm and down bottles of aspirin to dull the throbbing, I usually forget to be grateful for pain. But at that very moment, pain is alerting my body to the danger, mobilizing anti-infection defenses around the wound and preventing me from further compounding the injury. Pain demands the attention which is crucial to my recovery.

He jests at scars who never felt a wound.
William Shakespeare

* 3 *

Painless
Hell

I f we have pain, we don't want it. Knowing medical details of its value still won't convince us emotionally that it is a desirable, necessary part of life. But a trip I took in the spring of 1976 indelibly impressed upon me an appreciation for pain. I spent a week with Dr. Brand, the crusader for pain.

Dr. Brand has a special interest in the pain network: he has spent most of his life among people with leprosy who are daily being destroyed because they have a defective pain system. The word "leprosy" conjures up exaggerated images of stubby fingers, ulcerated wounds, missing legs, distorted facial features. Literature and movies such as *Ben Hur* and *Papillon* (frequently inaccurate) have conditioned us to view leprosy, or Hansen's disease,* as one of the most cruel diseases imaginable.

Hansen's disease (HD) is cruel, but not at all the way other diseases are. It primarily acts as an anesthetic, numbing the pain cells of hands, feet, nose, ears, and eyes. Not so bad, really, one might think. Most diseases are feared *because* of their pain—what makes a painless disease so horrible?

Hansen's disease's numbing quality is precisely the reason such fabled destruction and decay of tissue occurs. For thousands of years people thought HD caused the ulcers on hands and feet and face which eventually led to rotting flesh and loss of limbs. Mainly through Dr. Brand's research, it has been established that in 99 percent of the cases, HD only numbs the extremities. The destruction follows solely because the warning system of pain is gone.

How does the decay happen? In villages of Africa and Asia, a person with HD has been known to reach directly into a charcoal fire to retrieve a dropped potato. Nothing in his body told him not to. Patients at Brand's hospital in India would work all day gripping a shovel with a protruding nail, or extinguish a burning wick with their bare hands, or walk on splintered glass. Watching them, Brand began formulating his radical theory that HD was chiefly anesthetic, and only indirectly a destroyer.

On one occasion, he tried to open the door of a little

---

*Patients vastly prefer the term Hansen's disease because it does not carry the social and moral stigma of "leprosy."

storeroom, but a rusty padlock would not yield. A patient—an undersized, malnourished ten-year-old—approached him, smiling.

"Let me try, sahib doctor," he offered and reached for the key. With a quick jerk of his hand he turned the key in the lock.

Brand was dumbfounded. How could this weak youngster out-exert him? His eyes caught a telltale clue. Was that a drop of blood on the floor?

Upon examining the boy's fingers, Brand discovered the act of turning the key had gashed a finger open to the bone; skin, fat, and joint were all exposed. Yet the boy was completely unaware of it! To him, the sensation of cutting his finger to the bone was no different from picking up a stone or turning a coin in his pocket.

The daily routines of life ground away at the HD patient's hands and feet, but no warning system alerted him. If an ankle turned, tearing tendon and muscle, he would adjust and walk crooked. If a rat chewed off a finger in the night, he would not discover it missing until the next morning.

_____ Visit to Carville _____

I saw firsthand the devastating results of a life without pain on my visit with Dr. Brand. He now works at one of the most remarkable institutions in this country, a "leprosarium" in Carville, Louisiana—the U.S. Public Health Service Hospital.

Because of the stigma of Hansen's disease, Carville is remote and extremely difficult to reach by land. The hospital is built on the site of a 112-year-old plantation, which at one time was surrounded by swamp. Land for the hospital was bought in the 1890s under the pretense of starting an ostrich farm, so neighbors would not suspect the buyers' true intent.

The hospital itself is spread out over 337 acres and includes a nine-hole golf course and a stocked lake in addition to modern treatment facilities. Barbed wire around Carville has come down now, and visitors are welcome.* Tours are even given three times daily.

A pleasant environment, buildings designed for wheelchair patients, the best medical care, free treatment with the newest drugs available—on the surface life at this shaded plantation setting seems almost enviable. The disease is under control now; most cases can be arrested in early stages. But one horrible aspect of Hansen's disease remains: the loss of pain sensation.

_____ **Lou's Dangerous Autoharp** _____

I am visiting a patient clinic at Carville. Two physical therapists, a nurse, and Dr. Paul Brand are seated in chairs arranged in a semicircle facing a TV screen. Today three patients with serious problems will be seen.

The first enters, a middle-aged Hawaiian man named Lou (not his real name). Lou has more visible deformities than most, since he came to Carville when HD was already advanced in him. His eyebrows and eyelashes are gone, which gives his face a naked, unbalanced appearance. His eyelids are paralyzed, so tears tend to

---

*Leprosy is such a dreaded word that it's been impossible to enlighten the public about the true nature of Hansen's disease. Carville patients explain that of all contagious diseases, Hansen's is probably least contagious and that 90 percent of all people are immune. Despite the close daily contact with infected patients, in ninety years of operation, only one person, a worker, has been known to contract HD at Carville. Having come from an endemic area, he was suspected of being latently infected before working at Carville.

overflow as though he were crying. Dr. Brand whispers to me that Lou is almost totally blind. The loss of pain was partially responsible: the surface of his eye stopped signaling the irritation and discomfort that called for blinking, and as his dulled eyelids blinked less frequently, Lou's eyes gradually dried up.*

Lou's feet are smooth stumps, with no visible toes. His hands are lined with deep cracks and scars from former ulcers. But his main problem is psychological— Lou feels a door has been shut between him and the world. Nearly blind, he can't perceive people. He has lost the sensation of touch and would not even feel it if he burned his hand or stepped on a nail. His last remaining good sense is hearing, and that is the source of his fear.

His voice trembling, Lou tells the group how much he loves the autoharp. He can strum the Hawaiian melodies of his childhood and dream of younger days. A devout Christian, he picks out hymns as praise to God, sometimes playing for his church. To play, Lou tapes the pick onto one spot on his finger which he claims still has some sensation. He can sense enough variation in pressure to know how to select the strings and strum them. But he is not sensitive enough to be alert to dangerous pressure. Hours of playing the autoharp have left calluses and ulcers on the thumb. He has been afraid

---

*Carville's most famous patient, Stanley Stein (author of *Alone No Longer*) went blind because of another cruel quirk of HD. Each morning he would wash his face with a hot washcloth. But neither his hand nor his face was sensitive enough to temperature to warn him that he was using scalding water. Gradually he destroyed his eyes with his daily washing.

to come to the clinic until now. *Can Dr. Brand find some way for him to continue playing without damaging his hand?* he asks, almost pleading in a thick accent.

The committee of doctors and physical therapists view Lou's hand on a TV monitor. They are using a thermogram, which translates body temperatures into gaudy colors. On a thermogram Lou's hand is outlined in a psychedelic blend of chartreuse, lemon-yellow, scarlet, and all shades in between. Green represents the coolest portions, violet nearly normal. Bright red is a danger sign—it shows infection is being fought internally. Yellow shows extreme danger.

The single most useful spot on Lou's thumb is easily visible. It's a yellow pinpoint of heat, because constant, wearing use has inflamed the area. The thermogram is science's best warning system for painless persons. Unfortunately, unlike pain, it detects danger *after* the period of stress, not during it. You and I would be highly conscious of an infected thumb. It would throb all day long until we stopped using it and treated it. But Lou has no such advantage. He never knows when he is worsening the spreading spot of infection in his thumb.

The committee designs a glove to fit Lou's hand, which will relieve some of the pressure of the autoharp pick. After he leaves, the nurse who works with Lou expresses pessimism. "Lou hates gloves. They call attention to his hands, and undoubtedly he won't have as much control over his pick. Probably he'll try it for a day, then throw it away."

Already Lou is withdrawing from people, losing contact with them as his senses of sight, hearing, and touch fade. Now his last great love—intimate self-expression through music—is threatened. He may return in a few weeks with a spreading infection which has caused permanent damage to his thumb. He may even lose the thumb. But treatment is voluntary. Without his own pain system to force him to act, Lou has the risky option of ignoring the thermogram's warning.

_____ **A Mop and a Shoe** _____

Another patient, a man with blue skin, enters the room. Hector speaks in a deep drawl; he comes from Texas, one of the few states in the U.S. where Hansen's disease is found. He has some resistance to the sulfone drugs most commonly used for treatment, and doctors have been trying a new drug for treatment which is a dye. That explains the large blotches of his skin which are shaded a muted blue. Hector gladly sacrifices normal appearance to halt HD's spread in his body.

The thermogram, though, quickly reveals a bright red danger in the webbing between Hector's right thumb and forefinger. A callus has hidden any external signs of infection. Quizzing him like detectives, Dr. Brand and the others ask Hector to trace his day's activities. How does he shave? Put on his shoes? Does he have a job? Does he play golf? Shoot pool?

Somewhere in his daily actions, Hector is grasping something too firmly between his thumb and forefinger. Unless they can find the faulty activity and ask him to stop, his hand will suffer more injury.

At last they find it. After his mild day's work as a canteen cashier, Hector helps in the cleanup. Every day he mops the floor to erase any spilled soft drinks or candy. The back and forth motion, coupled with Hector's inability to detect how hard he is squeezing the mop handle, have scarred tissue inside his thumb. The mystery is solved.

Hector thanks the group profusely. A physical therapist promises to ask Hector's supervisor to allow him to substitute some other activity.

One more patient comes in—Jose. In contrast to most people at Carville, Jose is dressed in the latest fashions. His doubleknit pants are a bright blue-and-red plaid, and his shirt has obviously been pressed at a cleaners. His shoes, too, are unlike the dull, black orthopedic shoes of most patients. They have a snappy, narrow-toe design and are polished to a high brown gloss.

Jose's shoes are, in fact, the problem. He dresses meticulously because he has a full-time job as a furniture salesman. Carville therapists have tried to convince Jose to wear less stylish, more helpful shoes, but he has always declined. His job and image are more important to him than even the loss of much of his feet.

When Jose removes his shoes and socks, his feet show the worst injury I have seen. There is not even one nub where his toes should be, just rounded stumps which he walks on. Thermograms graphically illustrate the problem. Without toes to cushion the effect of the heel-lifting upstep, Jose is systematically wearing down his stump, causing constant infection.

A normal person would automatically limp, or change walking styles, to break in a new pair of shoes. But Jose can't feel the danger signs. The committee talks with him at length about the problem, but Jose is politely unyielding. He will not wear Carville-made shoes, which look to him like training shoes. It would tip off his customers that something is wrong with him. His facial features and hands are almost normal—he won't let his feet betray him.

Finally, Dr. Brand calls in the shoemaker and asks him to make some adjustments on Jose's shoes which may relieve the pressure.

After the patients leave, Dr. Brand turns to me and says, "Pain—it's often seen as the great inhibitor which ropes off certain activities. But I see it as the great giver of freedom. Look at these men. Lou: we're desperately searching for a way to give him simple freedom to play an autoharp. Hector: he can't even mop a floor without harming himself. Jose: too proud for proper treatment, he's given a makeshift shoe which may keep him from losing even more of his feet. He can't dress nicely and walk normally; for that, he would need the gift of pain."

_____ **Painless People** _____

Carville and other HD hospitals around the world have the most concentrated groups of people who are destroying themselves without pain. But leprosy is not the only condition which muffles the sensation. Diabetics face similar dangers of loss of extremities. Alcoholics and drug addicts can dull their sensitivities (each winter alcoholics die of exposure in northern cities, their bodies numb to the biting cold). A few people are born with a bizarre defect called "congenital indifference to pain." They have a warning system of sorts, but, like Dr. Brand's flashing lights and audible signals, it doesn't hurt. To them, the sensation of touching a hot stove is the same as touching an asphalt driveway. For a child, especially, the danger is that he can interpret pain signals as pleasure signals and further harm himself.

One family told a grotesque story about their congenitally insensitive baby daughter who had just grown four teeth. The mother, hearing her laughing and cooing in the next room, went to her expecting to find some new game the child had discovered. The baby had bitten off the tip of her finger and was playing with the blood, making patterns with the drops. Without pain, she had lost the innate sense of self-protection. How do you explain the danger of matches, knives, and razor blades to children like this? One seven-year-old picked at her nose until her nostrils became ulcerated.

These people can undergo surgery without anesthesia, and they can impress their friends with painless feats, such as pushing a straight pin through their fingers. But their lives are marked with danger. An afflicted woman nearly lost her life because she developed a serious illness without feeling its warning symptom, a headache. Most suffer some kind of bone damage because of unrecognized abuse. They can sprain a wrist without knowing it, then continue to use the wrist at great detriment. One sixteen-year-old girl lost all ten of her fingers through neglect.

The congenitally insensitive must depend on clues which they learn. They can feel something, such as a tickling sensation. To respond, though, they have to consciously attend to the area involved. You or I would react immediately; they must concentrate on what action to take.

Examples of "painless hell" are numerous and tragic. They should make all of us discard the common notion that pain is an unpleasantness to be avoided at all costs. Generally, pain does not dampen life. More than anything, it frees us to enjoy normalcy on this planet. Without it, we would lead unbalanced, paranoid lives, encountering unknown dangers, never confident that we weren't destroying ourselves.

Medical textbooks had done much to convince me of pain's value before I visited Carville. Already I was beginning to see that, even in Claudia Claxton's case, pain was not the root problem—the disease was. Pain was merely informing her that cancer cells and cobalt rays were harming her body. Without pain, she might have died, unaware of the disease's presence.

The week at Carville left me with profound visual memories. Whenever I am tempted to curse God for pain, I remember Lou: his eyes running, his face scarred, unaware of anyone touching him, searching frantically for a way to keep his music, his last love in life.

The only safe environment for a painless person is to stay in bed all day...but even that produces bedsores.

Just realize, I am 69 and I have never seen a person die. I have never even been in the same house while a person died. How about birth? An obstetrician invited me to see my first birth only last year. Just think, these are the greatest events of life and they have been taken out of our experience. We somehow hope to live full emotional lives when we have carefully expunged the sources of the deepest human emotions. When you have no experience of pain, it is rather hard to experience joy.

George Wald
Nobel Prize winner

* 4 *

The Agony, Then the Ecstasy

I f you, too, could visit a leprosarium, you would probably never again question the important role of pain. Without it, life is a miserable succession of fears and dangers. Confronted with the physiological facts, most of us will admit that, yes, some pain is a useful and good thing.

Even more neglected than that aspect of pain, however, is the intimacy between pain and pleasure. The two sensations work together, often accompanying one another, sometimes becoming almost indistinguishable.

Not only is pain useful as a warning—it may also be an essential element in our richest experiences.

Does that sound odd? It should, for our modern culture barrages us daily with the opposite. We are told that pain is the antithesis of pleasure. If you feel a slight headache, battle it immediately with the appropriate-strength aspirin. If your nose barely drips, dry it up with a sinus decongestant. At the slightest cramp of constipation, visit a drugstore and select one of the candies, liquids, pills, or enemas.

We moderns have isolated ourselves from a world which claims pain as an integral part of it. In all of history except very recent times pain was a normal, everyday occurrence which was taken for granted in any balanced view of life. Now it is an adjunct, an intruder we must excise.

Urbanized society removes us from the daily cycle of pain and death in the animal world. How many people whom you know would wring the neck of a chicken? It's not easy. It takes strength and quick coordination to twist the neck with a quick snap. But the process teaches you something about life. The featherless, man-ureless, bloodless hunks of meat which lie shrink-wrapped on a grocery-store counter teach nothing about life—they remove it from us.

Let me quickly add that I buy shrink-wrapped chicken, and my office is air-conditioned to ease the discomfort in summer. I also wear shoes to avoid the unevenness of walking on gravel, and I wear a tennis glove while playing to prevent blisters and calluses. I do these things deliberately, gladly, for they make my life more comfortable. But they also help to insulate me. Abundant luxuries and conveniences give me a perspective on the world and on pain which was not shared by any other century in history and is still unrealized by two-thirds of the current world population. I, along with most Americans, tend to see pain as a sensation which can and should be mastered by technology. Our distorted viewpoint helps foster the myth that pain and pleasure are diametrically opposed: our life styles murmur it to us every day.

Buzzed Brains

A bioengineer I talked with in Louisiana likens the brain to an amplifier. Connected to it are a dazzling collection of input sources. Instead of phono turntables and tape decks we have the senses of touch, vision, hearing, etc. When a sense starts to fade, the brain automatically turns up the volume control. Sometimes a person with Hansen's disease will not detect a loss of sensation until it is completely gone, because his brain has compensated by increasing the volume until the sense has died.

Modern culture saddens me because it is constantly turning up the volume. We have ears: they are bombarded with decibels until the subtle tones are lost forever. We have eyes: the world confronts them with Day-Glow and phosphorescent paints until a sunset or butterfly pales in comparison. We have noses: packaged chemical smells come in magazines, so that we need only scratch and sniff. We spray ourselves with a variety of odors and spew tons of foul particles into the air, so that some of us have no idea how the natural world should smell.

It is not enough to walk alongside a swamp and listen to the frogs and crickets, watch the turtles plop like bloated submarines into the water, and smell the faint scent of wildflowers. It is not enough, even, to visit the American West, where nature is far from subtle. There, rocks loom capriciously from the horizon in gargantuan shapes; waterfalls assault the senses with a deafening roar, a pelting spray of ice water, and a visual display of fast-motion beauty; cartoonish animals such as moose and beavers await discovery.

Instead, we experience all those things vicariously, slumped in front of a flickering TV set with its unnatural colors. Some in our culture use drugs to heighten perception; they sit alone, enjoying an internal psychedelic light show, their emotions shifting gears like a high-speed racer.

Teen-agers use the word "stoned" for people so blitzed with sensations that they are dulled almost senseless. I prefer the word "buzzed," following the brain/amplifier analogy.

It is too easy for us to perceive the sensations of life as something which must be done *to* us. We don't see pleasure as something we reach out for and actively attain after struggle. If it involves pain, we abandon the search.

Annie Dillard wrote one of my favorite books, *Pilgrim at Tinker Creek*, which won 1975's National Book Award and a Pulitzer Prize. If you asked me what it's about, I would say, "Well, this lady lives by a creek, and she goes for walks in the woods and sees muskrats and caterpillars and things. There's really not much plot— just the way she reacts to those walks." But the book is remarkable because it shows a person who looks, and hears, and smells, *actively*. Her writing is not idyllic nature-worship; it plumbs the mysteries of pain and death in nature. Her discoveries are layers deeper than most of us ever get. She can make a walk in the woods far more staggering than a trip to Disneyland.

Our culture has tended to remove us from the world of active sensations, including those which involve pain.

_____ Beds of Coconut Matting _____

Like muscles, our senses can, through exercise, become more responsive. Some scientists theorize that our fingertips are so incredibly sensitive because from infancy we use them so much. Nerve endings can "improve." You can raise your own skin sensitivities by brushing your arm daily with a nylon brush. Eventually the arm will pick up a much wider range of pleasure and pain sensations.

For this reason, Dr. Brand, half in jest but half-seriously, suggested to me that babies should be raised on coconut matting rather than on down blankets. Surrounding babies with softness and neutral sensations stifles their nerve-growth and limits their range of interpreting the world. Brand also confesses his wife discouraged him from stringing his children's playpens with barbed wire. Cruel? It would merely train a child to accept a world where certain things (like hot stoves) are off-limits and painful. The more you coddle children, he says, the more you set them up for an insulated, sensation-starved life.

Going barefoot, for example, helps to vary skin sensation, especially if you walk on the sand of a beach or on grass. The subtle variations in a lawn's shape and texture feed the brain with needed sensory input, which is vital for the brain's development. French scientists constructed chambers where people could live isolated from all external stimulation. They found that to function properly, humans must be bombarded with outside stimuli. Without it, the subjects became disoriented and restless, and even experienced hallucinations.[1]

It is easy to forget that the *same nerve sensors and pathways which carry messages of pain to the brain also carry messages of pleasure*. The sensation of itch (unpleasant) and the sensation of tickle (pleasant) are the same stimuli, the only difference being that tickling involves the motion of something acting on you—a feather pulled over skin, or a finger wiggled on a sensitive spot. The nerve sensors are the same; we simply interpret one action as pleasant and one as unpleasant. Some pains, such as prick-pain which can stop the itching of a mosquito bite, or the aches of stretching after a hard day of work, are closer to being pleasant than unpleasant.

The sensors in your fingers which alert you to heat, or a slight electric shock, or a rough surface, are the same sensors which convey to you the feel of velvet or satin. The sensors that give you sexual pleasure are the same sensors which carry messages of alarm to the brain.

People who enjoy hot baths often run the water hotter than they can stand it. They wait a few minutes, then gingerly lower a hand or leg into the water. Ouch! A stinging shot of pain. They withdraw, then try again. The pain is less this time. It gradually feels good. Then they lower other parts of their body into the bath.

The process of lowering your body into a tub full of very hot water perfectly illustrates the close association between pain and pleasure. They mix, becoming indistinguishable. Cells quickly adjust, and the water which seconds before had alerted your brain to a danger substance soon becomes a soothing, relaxing environment.

_____ **Raisins in the Sierra** _____

This close association between pain and pleasure is not just true of the body. Human experience reflects the conjoined quality of life. Often intense pleasure comes only after prolonged struggle.

A friend of mine backpacks on long hikes in the High Sierra. The strenuous, tiring, activity taxes him to his physical limits. At the end of the day, he slumps exhausted into a sleeping bag and awakes to aches and bruises. Stumbling on loose rock and climbing across solid granite wear down his muscles, crack his fingers, and cause more pain.

In the middle of these experiences, my friend relates, his senses are affected. They seem to come alive. When he breathes in great gulps of air, he's more aware of the air. He notices things with his eyes and ears that he normally would overlook. Once, after an afternoon of hiking in the cold fog, he rummaged through his coat pockets for food. Running low on supplies, he could only spare a box of raisins. He casually opened the box and tossed the first raisin into his mouth. Incredible flavor flowed into the juices of his mouth. He ate another and another. They were like super-raisins, far more tasty and refreshing than any he had eaten at home.

The process of using his body and plugging into all his senses freed up a whole new level of pleasure awareness. The extraordinary, delicious taste of those raisins would never have been his without the strain and toil of clambering over rocks all day.

Lin Yutang describes an ancient Chinese philosophy in his book, *My Country and My People*: "To be dry and thirsty in a hot and dusty land—and to feel great drops of rain on my bare skin—ah, is this not happiness! To have an itch in the private part of my body—and finally to escape from my friends and to a hiding place where I can scratch—ah, is this not happiness!" In Yutang's long list of happiness experiences, almost every one combines pain with ecstasies.

The sensations of hunger and thirst can lead to torment. But without them, could we have been blessed with the delights of taste?

Athletes know well this strange brotherhood between pain and ecstasy. Watch an Olympic weight lifter. He approaches the steel bar with its bulging wheels of weight. He takes deep breaths, grimaces, flexes his muscles. Reaching down, he gives a few preparatory tugs to limber up. Then he squats, tightens all the muscles of his body in one mighty reflex, and begins to lift. Oh, the pain in a weight lifter's face. Every millisecond it takes him to jerk the weight to his shoulders and raise it over his head is etched in agony on his face. Muscles are screaming for relief.

If he succeeds, he drops the bar with a tremendous *thong* on the floor and jumps in the air, his hands clasped above his head. Absolute agony and absolute ecstasy occur within two seconds. One would not have existed without the other. Ask the weight lifter what he thought of the pain—he will stare at you, bewildered. He has already forgotten, for it has been swallowed up in pleasure.

A Three-Year Prelude

On a higher level, most worthwhile human accomplishments involve a long history of struggle. Would the pleasure be possible without the painful process? The sculptures and paintings of Michelangelo involved years of pain and misery. Anyone who has accomplished something worthwhile in a house, such as building cabinets or planting a garden, knows this truth. The pleasure, coming after the pain, absorbs it. Jesus used childbirth as an analogy: nine months of waiting, intense labor, then absolute ecstasy (John 16:21).

I talked once with Robin Graham, the youngest person in history to sail around the world alone.* He started as an immature, searching kid of sixteen. During his three-year voyage, he was smashed broadside by a violent ocean storm, saw his mast snapped in two by a wave, and barely missed total destruction in a waterspout.

He went through such despair in the Doldrums, a windless, currentless portion of the ocean around the Equator, that he completely gave up, doused his boat with kerosene, and set it on fire. (He quickly changed his mind and jumped back in to extinguish the fire with his hands.)

After three years, Robin sailed into the Los Angeles harbor and was greeted by boats, banners, crowds, newsmen, honking cars, and blasts from steam whistles. The joy of returning was far different from any other sailing experience he had known. He would never have felt those emotions returning from a pleasure outing off

*His story was made famous in three *National Geographic* articles, then in the book and movie *Dove*.

the coast. The pain and agony of his round-the-world trip made possible the exultation of his triumphant return. He left a sixteen-year-old kid and returned a nineteen-year-old man.

Impressed by the mental health which self-accomplishment could bring, Robin immediately bought a farm plot in Kalispell, Montana, and built a cabin from hand-cut logs. Publishers and movie agents tried to entice him with round-the-country trips, the fame of talk shows, and the comfort of fat expense accounts, but Robin declined them all.

The Backdrop of Courage

There's a corollary to the pain/pleasure principle in the Christian concept of service. The genius of Christianity is that true fulfillment is found, not through comfortable ego-fulfillment, but through painful, tedious service. Mother Theresa, among the dregs of Calcutta, finds an entirely new level of peace and happiness.

The leprosarium in Carville, Louisiana, was first bought by the state, which promised to develop it. But the state could find no one willing to clear the roads, repair the slave cabins, or drain the swamps. No one would work near people with Hansen's disease. Finally, an order of nuns, the Sisters of Charity, chose to nurse those with HD. The nuns ended up digging ditches, repairing the building, and making the place livable, all the while glorifying God and bringing joy to the patients. They learned perhaps the deepest level of pain/pleasure association in life, that of sacrificial service.

Pain cannot be extracted from life's experiences and roundly condemned. A knee-jerk reaction against God for allowing pain is futile. It is too closely woven into the fabric of our sensations, and often it is a necessary step to pleasure and fulfillment.

When I am old, I hope I do not die between sterile sheets, hooked up to a respirator in a germ-free environment. I hope I'm on a tennis court, straining my heart with one last septuagenarian overhead smash, or perhaps huffing and puffing along a trail to Lower Yosemite Falls for one last feel of the spray against my wrinkled cheek.

If I spend my life searching for happiness through drugs, comfort, and luxury, it will elude me. "Happiness recedes from those that pursue her." Happiness will come upon me unexpectedly, as a by-product, a surprising bonus for something I have invested myself in. And, most likely, that investment will include much pain. It is hard to imagine pleasure without it.

It was only when I lay there on rotting prison straw that I sensed within myself the first stirrings of good. Gradually, it was disclosed to me that the line separating good and evil passes, not through states, nor between classes, nor between political parties either, but right through every human heart, and through all human hearts. So, bless you, prison, for having been in my life.

Alexander Solzhenitsyn
The Gulag Archipelago

* 5 *

The Stained Planet

Consider earth, our home. Let your eyes absorb the brilliant hues and delicate shadings of a sunset or a rainbow. Dig your toes into sand and feel the rolling foam and spray of a dependable ocean tide. Visit a museum and study the abstract designs on butterflies—10,000 wild variations, far more staggering than the designs of modern abstract painters, all compressed into tiny swatches of flying fabric. Belief in a loving God is easy among these good things.

Yet the sun which lavishes the sky with color can bake African soil into dry, cracked glaze, dooming millions of people. The steady, pounding rhythm of surf can, when fomented by a storm, crash in as a twenty-foot wall of death, obliterating towns and villages. And the harmless swatches of color which spend their lifetimes fluttering among flowers are snatched and destroyed in the daily ferocity of nature's life cycles. The world, though God's showplace, is also a rebel fortress. It is a good thing, bent.

Consider man. The country which produced Bach, Beethoven, Luther, Goethe, and Brahms also gave us Hitler, Eichmann, and Goering. The country which fathered the Constitution of the United States brought us slavery and the Civil War. In all of us, streaks of brilliance, creativity, and compassion jostle with streaks of deceit, selfishness, and cruelty.

And so it is with pain.

Up close, pain may seem a trusted, worthy friend. The nervous system, so obviously stamped with genius, can be admired like an exquisite Raphael painting. From the nearsighted viewpoint of a bioengineer, the pain network surely appears as one of God's greatest works.

Pain, however, comes to our attention not through the microscope, but through throbs of torment. If you relate each warning signal to its specific cause, the pain network seems well-functioning and good. But if you step back and see all humanity, a writhing, starving, bleeding, cancerous progression of billions of people marching toward death... there, a problem arises.

Philosophers love the larger, farsighted view which discusses "the sum total of human suffering," as if all human pain could be sucked out and extruded into one great vial to present to God: "Here is all the pain and suffering of Planet Earth. How do You account for this mass of misery?" It is a dilemma. Pain may have been intended as a smooth, efficient warning system, but something about this planet is in dreadful revolt. Suffering is raging out of control.

Later in this book you will meet people with broken spinal cords and Jewish survivors of the Holocaust. These are the people we must face head-on. No amount of mushy rationalizing can resolve their piercing questions. And these are the people who raise the question "Where is God when it hurts?" most shrilly. If our faith cannot answer them, then we have nothing to say to a broken world.

The problem of pain includes more than the reflexes of nerve cells. We have seen examples of "good pain" with its warnings and protections, but what about the side effects of pain? What of the psychological overtones as it wears down the soul, fueling bitterness and despair? Why are some people cursed with arthritis, cancer, or birth defects while others are healthy? Why so many cases of intense "bad pain" scattered throughout life?

Though some of us escape through life without intense physical suffering, everyone I know has some pain that won't go away. It may be a personality quirk, a broken relationship, a gnawing guilt...regardless, it keeps reappearing and wearing down our sense of contentment.

To look at suffering we must step back from the microscope, where we have seen pain cells obediently, beautifully responding to stimuli. Rather, we must look full in the face of agonized human beings. The question "Where is God when it hurts?" becomes, "Where is God when it won't stop hurting?" How can God allow such intense, unfair pain?

_____ **The Wild Animal** _____

The Bible traces the entrance of suffering and evil into the world to a grand but terrible quality of human beings—freedom. What makes us different from cavorting porpoises, roaring lions, and singing birds? Humans alone have been released from the stereotyped, instinctual behavior of an animal species. We have true, self-determining choice. We can even manipulate and control our environment.

Free man, however, introduced something new to the planet—a rebellion against the original design. We only have slight hints of the way earth was meant to be, but we do know that humanity has broken out of the mold. "We talk of wild animals," says Chesterton, "but man is the only wild animal. It is man that has broken out. All other animals are tame animals; following the rugged respectability of the tribe or type."[1]

Man is wild because he alone, on this speck of rock called earth, stands up to God, shakes his fist, and says, "I do what I want to do because I want to do it, and God had better leave me alone."[2] We've built a wall separating us from God. Inside the wall, we live pretty much as we please. Sometimes we follow the rules God laid out: the way of love and peace and goodness. Sometimes we don't.

Most remarkably, God listens. He allows man the freedom to do what he wants, defying all the rules of the universe (at least for a time). "In making the world, He set it free. God had written, not so much a poem but rather a play; a play He had planned as perfect, but which had necessarily been left to human actors and stage-managers, who have since made a great mess of it."[3]

Discussion of the universal aspects of suffering must begin here. Do not judge God solely by the world, just as you would not judge Picasso by his Blue Period alone. The world is in revolt. God has already hung a "Condemned" sign above the earth, and He has promised judgment. That this world full of evil and suffering still exists at all is an example of God's mercy, not His cruelty.

Somehow, pain and suffering were unleashed as necessary companions to misused human freedom. When man chose against God, his free world was forever spoiled.

_____ **Another Way?** _____

By a commitment to human freedom, God imposed certain limits on Himself. Whenever a creator enters a medium, he is limited by that medium. For example, to borrow an analogy from C.S. Lewis, God made wood, a useful product. It bears the fruit of trees, supports leaves to provide shade, and shelters birds and squirrels. Even taken from the tree, wood is useful. Men use it to heat themselves, to build their houses and furniture. The properties of wood—hardness, impliability, flammability—allow it to perform these useful functions. But as soon as you bequeath a material with those properties to a world peopled by free men, you inject inherent danger. A man can take a hunk of wood and, because of its firmness, use to to bash the head of another man.

God could, I suppose, reach down each time and change the properties of wood into those of sponge, so that the club would bounce off lightly. But that is not what He is about in the world. He has set into motion fixed laws which can, in fact, be perverted to evil by our misguided freedom. The pain network, although a useful gift for us, is likewise subject to abuse and extreme suffering on this earth.

Given the parameters of protecting man's free will, could God have done it another way? Could He have maintained some of the benefits of the pain network without the disadvantages?

There is some question as to whether any warning system that did not include suffering would work. As Dr. Brand's experiments and the experience of painless people show, it is not enough for us to be alerted when pain is present. It must *hurt*, so as to demand action.

But there is a further question—would it have been good for God to create a painless world, or one with less suffering? The Bible clearly demonstrates that some things are more awful to God than the pain of His children. Consider the psychological pain Abraham underwent when God asked him to kill his son Isaac. Or the awesome pain of Himself becoming man and bearing the sins of the world. Skeptics have cited these incidents as examples of God's lack of compassion. To me, they prove that some things—like declaring the truth—are more important on God's agenda than the suffering-free world for even His most loyal followers.

One can argue all day about whether God could have permitted our world one less virus or three less bacteria. None of us knows the answer to those questions, or even to the prior question of how a specific virus entered the world. (Was it a direct creative activity of God?) But the practical result of suffering is consistent with the Bible's view of Planet Earth. It is a stained planet, and suffering reminds us.

_____ **The Megaphone** _____

What can God use to speak loudly enough so we'll pay attention? What will convince us that this earth is *not* running the way God's creation is supposed to run?

C.S. Lewis introduced the phrase "pain, the megaphone of God." It's an apropos phrase, because pain does shout. When I stub my toe or twist an ankle, pain shouts to my brain that something is wrong.

Similarly, the existence of suffering on this earth is, I believe, a scream to all of us that *something is wrong*. It halts us and makes us consider other values.

We could (some people do) believe that the purpose of life here is to be comfortable. Enjoy yourself, build a nice home, engorge good food, have sex, live the good life. That's all there is.

But the presence of suffering complicates that philosophy. It's much harder to believe that the world is here just so I can party when a third of its people go to bed starving each night. It's much harder to believe the purpose of life is to feel good when I see teen-agers smashed on the freeway. If I try to escape the idea and merely enjoy life, suffering is there, haunting me, reminding me of how hollow life would be if this world were all I'll ever know.

Sometimes murmuring, sometimes shouting, suffering is a "rumor of transcendence" that the entire human condition is out of whack. Something is wrong with a life of wars and violence and insults. We need help. He who wants to be satisfied with this world, who wants to think the only reason for living is to enjoy a good life, must do so with cotton in his ears; the megaphone of pain is a loud one.

It is this aspect of Christianity which made G.K. Chesterton say, "The modern philosopher had told me again and again that I was in the right place, and I had still felt depressed even in acquiescence. But I had heard that I was in the wrong place, and my soul sang for joy, like a bird in spring." Optimists had told him the world was the best of all possible worlds, but he couldn't accept that. Christianity made sense to him because it freely admitted that this is a stained, marred planet.

Once he stumbled upon this perspective, Chesterton found that

> good was not merely a tool to be used, but a relic to be guarded, like the goods from Crusoe's ship—even that had been the wild whisper of something originally wise, for, according to Christianity, we were indeed the survivors of a wreck, the crew of a golden ship that had gone down before the beginning of the world.
>
> But the important matter was this, that it entirely reversed the reason for optimism. And the instant the reversal was made it felt like the abrupt ease when a bone is put back in the socket. I had often called myself an optimist, to avoid the too evident blasphemy of pessimism. But all the optimism of the age had been false and disheartening for this reason, that it had always been trying to prove that we fit in to the world. The Christian optimism is based on the fact that we do not fit in to the world.[4]

You may accuse the Christian doctrine of suffering's origin—that it came as a result of man's aborted freedom—of being weak and unsatisfying. But at least, as Chesterton notes, the concept of a great-but-fallen world squares with what we know of reality. Some other religions try to deny that pain exists, or to rise above it. But suffering is consistent with the Christian view of the universe that reveals our home as the stained planet.

Pain, God's megaphone, can drive me away from Him. I can hate God for allowing such misery. Or, on the other hand, it can drive me to Him. I can believe Him when He says this world is not all there is, and take the chance that He is making a perfect place for those who follow Him on painwracked earth.

_____ Intensive-Care Wards _____

If you once doubt the megaphone value of suffering, visit the intensive-care ward of a hospital. It's unlike any other place in the world. All sorts of people will pace the lobby floors. Some are rich, some poor. There are beautiful, plain, black, white, smart, dull, spiritual, atheistic, white-collar, and blue-collar people. But the intensive-care ward is the one place in the world where none of those divisions makes a speck of difference, for all those people are united by a single, awful thread—their love for a dying relative or friend. You don't see sparks of racial tension there. Economic differences, even religious differences fade away. Often they'll be consoling one another or crying quietly. All are facing the rock-bottom emotions of life, and many of them call for a pastor or priest for the first time ever. Only the megaphone of pain is strong enough to bring these people to their knees and make them reconsider life.

John Donne, a seventeenth-century poet, experienced great pain. Because he married the daughter of a disapproving lord, he was fired from his job as assistant to the Lord Chancellor, yanked from his wife, and locked in a dungeon. (This is when he wrote that succinct line of despair, "John Donne/Anne Donne/Undone.") Later, he endured a long illness which sapped his strength almost to the point of death.

In the midst of this illness, Donne wrote a series of devotions on suffering which rank among the most poignant meditations on the subject. In one of these, he considers a parallel: The sickness which keeps him in bed forces him to think about his spiritual condition. The parallel is apt. We ignore the megaphone of God—physical pain—which is repeating over and over how sick and needy we are, both physically and spiritually.

_____ Roger's Rescues _____

I once found a modern-day example of the megaphone value of pain when I interviewed an eighteen-year-old high school student who worked for Search and Rescue, a volunteer outfit which responds to outdoor emergencies. Roger Bowlin was chosen for the Seattle squad despite his youth because he had extraordinary athletic talents and good first-aid training. He observed the impact of pain on the people he rescued.

Weekend after weekend, Roger and his partner went through harrowing experiences. Once they climbed on a live glacier on the face of Mount Sloan, searching for a missing hiker. Roger could hear the dangerous sounds that mark a glacier's advance: low rumbles and piercing cracks like rifle shots. He saw tiny crevasses yawn open into yard-wide caverns. Retreating for their own safety, the two abandoned the search, and the hiker was never found.

On another occasion, Roger was called to hunt for a suicide victim on an island in Puget Sound. She had left a suicide note and disappeared. Roger found the body lying in a pasture, behind her home, next to a picture of her husband. A thick trail of hardened blood led to slit marks on her wrist.

"I remember another body vividly," Roger told me. "She'd been raped and thrown into the ice-cold Sound. The white body was washed up on a midstream sand bar. I remember how white she looked—her skin was all wrinkled and stiff. Feeling a dead body, thinking what she must have been through and how just hours before she was a normal person like me—it shook me horribly. I kept wanting to talk about it to friends."

Roger found that few people would talk about death and tragedy. "I couldn't believe it. Almost no one wanted to talk about death and how to be prepared for it, and how God fits in. People were very comfortable discussing the weather or clothes or Monday-night football. But no one wanted to talk about the things that really matter."

Eventually Roger became a Christian. The Christian view of the world—that it is a tragic, bloody place and that we need to be restored to God—was the only one that made sense to him. He admits now that, except for the haunting effects of the tragedies he encountered, he might never have come to God. Suffering—not even his own, rather, the suffering of others—forced him to consider life's values. He saw that his life was incomplete; he needed help to reorder it.

As a child turning to a father, Roger turned to God

for help in changing his life. That, I believe, is the mega-phone value of suffering. It is a general message to all of humanity. Is it a specific message? ("You're suffering *because* you did this.") That's the question of the next chapter. But generally, I think, God uses pain to tell us to trust Him, as a child trusts a father. Sometimes on the surface God seems unfair, or callous to our cries for help. But He hears them. As a Father, He hurts with us.

It is hard to be a child. We think we are big enough to run our own world without such messy things as pain and suffering to remind us of our dependence. We think we are wise enough to make our own decisions about morality. To live rightly without the megaphone of pain blaring in our ears.

We are wrong. The Garden of Eden story proves that. Man, in a world without suffering, chose against God.

And so we who have come after Adam have a choice. We can trust God. Or we can blame Him, not ourselves, for the world.

Only a personal God can be asked by the rebel for a personal accounting.

Albert Camus
The Rebel

* 6 *

What Is God Trying to Tell Us?

Flanked by weeping relatives, a Spanish-American couple sat in the shimmering heat of Sutter Cemetery, holding hands and staring dully at the bronze coffin that held the remains of their 17-year-old son Bobby. Six of Bobby's classmates placed their white carnation boutonnieres on the coffin. Bobby's young niece threw herself on the coffin and sobbed brokenly. Several in the large crowd also cried. Bobby's father silently shook his head a couple of times as though he had been struck, then moved woodenly with his wife toward the green limousine at the head of the long cortege.

In the same cemetery Mrs. Harry Rosebrough watched dry-eyed as her son was buried. He had died on his 16th birthday. Pamela Engstrom, wearing a blue-and-white gingham dress—a gift from her mother—had died the day after her 18th birthday. The victims also included twins Carlene and Sharlene Engle, 18, who loved to sing songs composed by their mother, "Wake and Smile in the Sunshine" and "Take Pride in America." After the funeral, Sharlene's dusty Ford station wagon was parked across the street from her home. A FOR SALE sign was in the window.

So it was [in Yuba City, California, in June, 1976] as 15,000 citizens mourned their dead. A bus bearing 53 members of the local high school choir and chaperon Christina Estabrook had ripped through 72 feet of guard-rail as it turned onto an exit ramp. The bus plunged 21½ feet to the ground. It landed on its top, wheels still spinning and roof crushed down to the seats.

Blood dripped on scattered sheets of choir music. "I heard someone scream 'Oh my God' from the front of the bus," sobbed Kim Kenyon, a 16-year-old junior whose girl friend was killed in the seat beside him. Added Perry Martin, 18, the choir's chief tenor: "Everything was a tangle of weeping and moaning and of scattered arms and legs." The final toll: 29 dead and 25 injured.

The boys and girls had gone through junior high school together. They had all performed together in "Fiddler on the Roof" earlier this year. Only three weeks from graduation, many of them had gone to their prom on the previous Saturday. Now their friends dazedly shuffled through Yuba City High School, pausing disconsolately from time to time at the principal's window *to read the daily notice that listed the condition of the injured. Said Karen Hess, 18, president of the student body: "This is the first time that most of us have ever had close friends die."*[1]

(Reprinted from *Time*, 7 June 1976.)

_____ **Why Yuba City?** _____

Why not Salina, Kansas ... or Clarkston, Georgia ... or Ridgewood, New Jersey?

Why the high-school choir? Why not the band ... or the debate team ... or the football team?

Why did those twenty-nine kids deserve a grisly mass highway death? Was God trying to tell them something? Or was He giving a lesson to their parents and friends?

If you were a teen-ager in Yuba City High School, you couldn't avoid those questions. If you had survived the bus accident as a passenger, you couldn't help wondering why you had lived when friends had died. Soon after a bloody tragedy like the Yuba City bus wreck, the questions snarl to the surface—some bitter, some anguished.

If anything, the questions seem harder to Christians. If you believe in a world of chance, what difference does it make whether Yuba City's bus or Salina's bus crashes? But if you believe in a world ruled by a powerful God who loves you tenderly—then it makes an awful difference.

Does our God reach down, slightly twist the wheels of school buses, and watch them carom through guardrails? Does He draw a red pencil line through a map of Indiana to plan the exact path a tornado should take? *There, hit that house, kill that six-year-old, but hop up and skip this next house.* Does God jostle the earth, playing with tidal waves, earthquake tremors, and hurricanes...squashing men out like cigarette butts? Is that how He rewards and punishes us, His helpless victims?

Posing the questions may sound sacrilegious. But they've haunted me and other Christians I know. And they've been tossed at me like spears by scoffing friends.

That God speaks to the human race in general through the megaphone of pain is one thing. But pain never comes to us in general. It comes in piercing, specific jolts. And so, I wonder: what is God trying to tell me by this strep throat? By my friend's death? Is He responsible? Does He have a specific message for me, or for the Yuba City survivors?

Pain has value in protecting our bodies—almost everyone grants that. Suffering even has some moral value in pointing to our temporary, needful condition on the Stained Planet; most Christians, at least, can accept that. However, most of the mental turmoil about pain and suffering hinges, I think, on this turbulent issue of *cause*. If God is truly in charge, somehow connected to all the world's suffering, why is He so capricious, unfair? Is He the cosmic Sadist who delights in watching us squirm?

At a banquet, a guest next to me referred to a recent earthquake in South America. "Did you know that a much lower percentage of Christians died in the earthquake than non-Christians?" he asked with utter sincerity. I wondered about the Christians who *were* killed—what had they done to deserve being cast in with the vulnerable pagans? And I wondered about the hint of smugness in his remark—like the old Colosseum scores: Christians 4, Gladiators 3.

How does God fit into this world He has made for us? Does He hover close above us, reaching in now and then to break an arm, cause a tragic death, unleash a flood? Or does He silently let the world slump along with its wars, tragedies, and violent history?

_____ **What the Bible Says** _____

If you search the Bible for an answer to the question of "Who did it?" you come away with mixed answers. A cursory glance at the Old Testament seems to indicate that, yes, God did intervene regularly in human history. He most often did so for consistent reasons: to reward the good and punish the wicked. Sometimes He employed suffering, even causing people's deaths. He caused armies to lose battles, just to teach them a lesson.

The prophets are full of warnings about suffering. But look closer. Whenever they pronounced doom, they first called out a list of sins which would bring on the doom. Amos limned all the gross sins of Israel's pagan neighbors before delivering God's judgment on them. Jeremiah, Habakkuk, Hosea, Ezekiel—they all spelled out impressive lists of sin and wickedness which occasioned Israel's punishment. And when they offered hope that God might restrain Himself, they always tied it to repentance. _If_ Israel repented and turned back to God, God's hand would be stayed. If she continued in rebellion, she would be crushed. So the judgment was clearly from God, but it was not capricious and unjust. It was consistent, and came with much warning.

The Psalms, too, are full of the reward/punishment kind of thinking. David anxiously beseeched God to punish his enemies for injustice, while rewarding him for his own faithfulness.

(Some good reasons have been offered to explain why the Old Testament so repeatedly presents this philosophy of "Do good, get rewarded; do bad, get punished." Some say the style was necessary to accomplish God's goals in Old Testament history. God was working in the world to establish a *nation* of His own select people, which would stand out in pure contrast to the rest of the world and would prepare for the coming Messiah. Thus, He was actively involved in human historical events. God's long-range plan, of course, was redemption of the world through Christ. But as one of the steps in accomplishing that plan, God needed to establish a beachhead of righteousness and justice. When Israel rebelled against the plan, He punished.)

Crudely put, the Old Testament conception of God is as an infrequent intervenor. Though He caused miracles and changes in the natural order of the world, He usually did so for a particular purpose, after considerable warning. Still, His interventions were the exception, not the rule. One need only read the bloody history of persecuted prophets and godly men to realize that God intervened rarely. The New Testament, however, seems to pull away from the Old Testament pattern of reward/punishment, possibly because of a shift in God's manner of acting in the world.

_____ **God on Earth** _____

With the coming of Jesus, something unprecedented and unfathomable took place. God fully entered human history. He was no longer "out there," sometimes dipping into history to change things. He suddenly resided in the body of a human on Planet Earth. How did that affect the pattern? What did He do on earth? Jesus performed supernatural miracles (none for punishment), but He usually used them as illustrations of some deeper truth. John's Gospel calls them "signs."

At times Jesus seemed reluctant to intervene, telling His followers He performed the signs only because they had need of them. Often He told His disciples and others not to spread the word of His miracles, to keep them quiet.

On certain occasions Jesus deliberately elected not to intervene in the natural order of things. For example, He chose not to call down angels to deliver Him from His most painful hour, before death.

Was Jesus saying to us that it is not good for God to intervene in our world on a day-to-day basis? The important thing, the kingdom of heaven—isn't that a kingdom of the spirit to be worked out inside the hearts and minds of men, not by an external, spectacular display of God's power?

How did Jesus deal with the question "Who is responsible for suffering?" Again, there are mixed answers. In Luke 13:16, for example, He declared that Satan caused the pain of a woman bound in disease for eighteen years. Yet in the very same chapter, Jesus sidestepped the question of causality. Someone informed Him of an atrocity—the Roman governor Pilate had butchered Jews who were sacrificing in the temple. Jesus turned and said, "Do you think they were worse sinners than other men from Galilee?" He brought up another current tragedy—the death of eighteen men when the Tower of Siloam fell—and asked the same question. In effect, Jesus was hinting that these men had done nothing unusual to deserve their fates. They were the same as other men. Perhaps the tower simply fell because it was built poorly. (I think Jesus would have replied similarly to the Yuba City tragedy: "Do you think they were worse sinners than other teen-agers?" Perhaps the bus crashed because of driver error or mechanical failure.)

In John 9, Jesus refuted the classic explanation of suffering. His followers pointed to a man who had been born blind. Clucking with pity, they asked, "Who sinned, this man or his parents?" In other words, why did he deserve blindness? Jesus answered bluntly, "Neither sinned." God was not "punishing" the man or his family through illness, as the disciples had assumed.

Is God the Cause?

Because of biblical hints like these, I doubt the view that God directly causes suffering to teach us specific lessons. He allows suffering to exist, and as His megaphone it can serve moral ends. But I can't believe He actively inflicts the pain for a specific purpose.

I once attended a funeral service for a teen-age girl killed in a car accident. Her mother wailed, "The Lord took her home. He must have had some purpose.... Thank You, Lord." I have been with sick Christian people who torment themselves with the question, "What is God trying to teach me?" Or, they may writhe, "How can I muster up enough faith to get rid of this illness? How can I get God to rescue me?"

Maybe they have it all wrong. Maybe God *isn't trying to tell us anything specific* each time we hurt. Pain and suffering are part and parcel of our planet, and Christians are not exempt. Half the time we know why we get sick: too little exercise, a poor diet, contact with a germ. Do we really expect God to go around protecting us whenever we encounter something dangerous?

As I look at the Bible, the evidence seems inconclusive. Sometimes God caused suffering for a specific reason—usually as a warning. Sometimes Satan caused it. In other cases, such as the Siloam disaster Jesus discusses, God wasn't intending any specific message. But one passage about suffering in the Bible—the most exhaustive treatment of the topic—has an unmistakable message. It comes in the Book of Job, smack in the middle of the Old Testament.

Job is the most righteous, spiritual man of his day. He loves God with all his heart. Remarkably, God even uses him as an example to prove to Satan how faithful some humans can be. If any man doesn't deserve suffering for his actions, it is Job.

But what happens? Incredibly, Job undergoes a wretched, unfair series of calamities. Raiders, fire, bandits, and a great wind take turns assaulting his ranch. Of all Job's great family and possessions, only his wife remains, and she is scant comfort!

In a second attack, Job breaks out in ulcerous, painful boils. In a matter of hours, his life has completely flip-flopped. All the terrors of hell have been poured out on him.

Job scratches himself and moans. The capricious suffering doesn't square with his belief in a loving, fair God.

In that setting, Job and his three friends discuss the mystery of suffering. Each of Job's friends fills the air with erudition. Boiled down, their arguments are virtually the same. *Job, God is trying to tell you something. You have suffered immeasurably, and there must be a reason. The only logical reason is that you have angered God by sinning. Therefore, confess your sin, and God will relieve your misery.* Job's only other option is suggested by his wife: curse God and die.

Job can't accept either choice. He knows that what has happened does not correspond to justice. In total despair, he even toys with the idea that God is a Sadist, who "delights in the calamity of the innocent" (Job 9:23).

Where is an answer for Job? The speeches of his three friends sound suspiciously like those of many Christians today. It is hard to find a defense of suffering, in this book or in any other, that is not contained in the conversations of Job's three friends. They seem devout, reverent men. Yet God calls all their elocution just "windy words."

Job resists accepting his friends' convincing arguments for several reasons. Knowing in his heart that he is righteous and does not deserve punishment, he maintains his position despite jabs such as "Are you more righteous than God?" He also observes that evil and good are not always punished and rewarded in this life. Thieves grow fat and prosper, while some holy men live painful, impoverished lives.

_____ **Painful Freedom** _____

Job also hints at an argument that to my mind effectively silences his three friends: the doctrine of man's freedom.

We often wish that everyone would "get what he deserved." Well, imagine a world in which punishment for sin came as swiftly as physical pain. If you touch a flame, you are punished instantly with a pain warning. What would it be like if you were punished for sin immediately?

Everyone in the world would clearly know what God expected. If they obeyed Him, they'd feel good and be rewarded, like a trained seal given a fish. If they disobeyed, they'd be electrically shocked. What a just, consistent world that would be.

There is, however, one huge flaw in such a neat world. It's not at all what God wants to accomplish on earth. There would be less true freedom in that world. We would act rightly because of our own immediate self-interest. Goodness would be tainted with selfish motives. We would love Him because of a programmed, inborn hunger, not because of a deliberate choice in the face of attractive alternatives.

It would be a B. F. Skinner, automaton world of action/response, action/response. In contrast, the Christian character described in the Bible is developed when we choose God and His ways in spite of temptation or impulses to do otherwise. John Wenham declares, "The highest goodness asks for no reward save that of knowing that it is doing God's will. It is really self-evident that if acts are to be truly virtuous, rewards and pains must not be obviously proportioned to deserts. To do right solely because it is right would scarcely be possible if the act were at once rewarded and the choice never costly."[2]

God wants us to freely choose to love Him, even when that choice involves pain—because we are committed to Him, not to our own good feelings and rewards. He wants us to cleave to Him, as Job did, even when we have every reason to hotly deny Him.

That, I believe, is the message of Job. Satan had

taunted God with the accusation that humans are not truly free, because God had weighted Job's rewards so he would choose in His favor. Was Job being faithful because God had allowed him such a prosperous life? The test proved he was not. Job is an eternal example of one who stayed faithful to God even though his world caved in and it seemed as though God Himself had turned against him. Job clung to God's justice when, apparently, he was the best example in history of God's alleged injustice. He did not seek the Giver because of His gifts; when all gifts were removed he still sought the Giver.

And so, even in the Old Testament, where suffering is so often identified with God's punishment, the sterling example of Job shines. He endured suffering which he did not deserve to demonstrate that God is ultimately interested in freely given love.

_____ **Free, Not Kept** _____

It is a hard truth, one at which great minds have stumbled. C. G. Jung went to strange lengths to explain away God's behavior in the Book of Job. He taught that God decided on the Incarnation and Jesus' death as a guilt reaction to the way He had treated Job. He entered the world in Jesus so that He could grow in moral consciousness.

Jung may be underestimating the premium God places on freely given love. Job's faithful response was so important to God that He allowed evident injustice to take place. Our freely given love is so important to God that He allows our planet to be an ulcer of evil in His universe—for a time.

Does God get off easy while leaving us to suffer? No.

He, timeless, could see from the beginning the streams of spittle on His face, could feel the ripping thud of hewn wood against a bleeding back, could hear the taunts of a jeering mob. Our freely given allegiance to Him, costing all that, was worth it to God.

Throughout the Bible, an analogy illustrating the relationship between God and His children recurs. God, the husband, is pictured as wooing the bride unto Himself. He wants her love. If the world were constructed so that every sin were punished with suffering and every good deed were rewarded with pleasure, the analogy would not hold. The closest analogy to that situation would be that of a "kept" woman, who is bought and spoiled and locked up in a room so that the lover can be sure she will be there when he returns. God does not "keep" His church for His own enjoyment. He loves us, gives Himself to us, and eagerly awaits our free response.

In summary, the Book of Job nails a coffin lid over one idea—the idea that every time we suffer, it's because God is punishing us or trying to tell us something specific. It just wasn't true of Job. Nobody deserved suffering less than Job, and yet few have suffered more. Sometimes God does send suffering as punishment (as in the ten plagues of Egypt), *but you cannot argue backwards*, as Job's friends tried to do, and assume that each incident of suffering can be linked to a specific failure. God Himself contradicted their accusations.

_____ **Fighting Plague and Tornados** _____

If the Bible were not so pronounced in denying the theory that all suffering is tied to our sins, if it did not paint the dilemma of Job in such universal, sweeping terms, tragedy could result. For, if we accept that all pain and suffering come from God as a lesson to us (as, for example, Islam does), the next logical step would be a resigned fatalism. Polio, cholera, malaria, plague, yellow fever—why should a person fight these if they are God's agents? Isn't He sending them to teach us a lesson?

The Christian church has, in fact, erred in this doctrine, and secular writers have insightfully exploited our weakness. In his novel *The Plague*, Albert Camus pictures a Catholic priest, Father Paneloux, torn by a paradox. Should he devote his energy to fighting the plague or to teaching his parishioners to accept it as from God? In a sermon, he concluded, "True, the agony of a child was humiliating to the heart and to the mind. But that was why we had to come to terms with it. And that, too, was why—and here Paneloux assured those present that it was not easy to say what he was about to say—since it was God's will, we, too, should will it. Thus and thus only the Christian could face the problem squarely. . . . We must go straight to the heart of that which is unacceptable, precisely because it is thus that we are constrained to make our choice. The sufferings of children were our bread of affliction, but without this bread our souls would die of spiritual hunger."[3]

Several years ago two researchers from the University of Chicago and Southern Illinois University studied victims of tornado damage across the country. They found that people in the South suffered a higher frequency of tornado-related deaths than Midwesterners, even after taking into account such factors as differences in building materials. After scrutinizing Alabamians and Illinoisans, the researchers concluded that Southerners, being more religious, had developed a fatalistic attitude toward disaster: "If it hits, it hits, and there's nothing I can do to stop it." In contrast, Midwesterners listened to weather reports, secured loose equipment, and went to a safe place to wait out tornado warnings.

"Alabamians were far more inclined than the Illinoisans were to see their lives as controlled by external forces. The Southerners saw God as actively involved in their lives rather than as a benevolent but noninterfering presence.

"Illinoisans tended to trust in technology to help them confront nature. But each Alabamian is on his own and faces the whirlwind alone with his God."[4]

If their conclusions are accurate, I take this as a dangerous perversion of Christian dogma. Suffering is not a direct act of God which we must swallow as punishment. Alabamians should listen to the weather service. Father Paneloux should have been on the front lines, arms linked with doctors, battling the plague. Jesus Himself spent His life on earth fighting disease and despair. He never hinted at fatalism or a resigned acceptance of suffering. As members of a stained planet, we have the right, even the obligation, to battle the negative side-effects of man's fall.

_____ Christian Merit Badges _____

Just as bad life does not always bring suffering, conversely, a good life does not exempt us from cruel pain. In fact, the Bible, especially the New Testament, offers little encouragement to those who would enlist in the Christian ranks to enjoy the sun and peace of a less painful world. If anything, the Christian's lot, at least in this life, is cast in threatening terms. James, Peter's

epistles, and Hebrews all admonish Christians to prepare to suffer. And among the roll call of the victorious
faithful in Hebrews 11 are those beaten to death,
whipped, chained, stoned, and starved in the desert.

Some Christians, notably those who stress God's miraculous healings, are puzzled by those parts of the
Bible which don't easily mesh with their beliefs. "Why
didn't God intervene more in Bible times? Why doesn't
He heal all Christians now?" they ask.

The questions flow from a persistent undercurrent of
wanting to avoid pain at all costs. We seem to reserve
our shiniest merit badges for those who have been
healed, featuring them in magazine articles and TV specials, with the frequent side-effect of causing unhealed
ones to feel as though God has passed them by. We
make faith not an attitude of trust in something unseen
but a route to get something *seen*—something magical
and stupendous, like a miracle or supernatural gift. Faith
includes the supernatural, but it also includes daily,
dependent trust in spite of results. True faith implies a
belief without solid proof—the evidence of things not
seen, the substance of things hoped for. God is not mere
magic.

Recently I watched a TV call-in healing program. The
biggest applause came when a caller reported his leg
was healed just one week before he was scheduled for
amputation. The audience shouted, and the emcee declared, "This is the best miracle we've had tonight!" I
couldn't help wondering how many amputees were
watching, forlornly wondering where their faith had
failed.

A sick person is not unspiritual. The Bible does not
pretend that a Christian should expect life to be easier,

more antiseptic, or safer than for a non-Christian.

The natural laws which rule this planet are, on the whole, good laws which fit the design God has for men and women. And becoming a Christian does not equip us with a germfree, hermetically sealed spacesuit to protect us from the dangers of earth.

If God halted all tragedies which involved Christians, it would insulate us from complete identification with the world. Paul begged for a "thorn in his flesh to be removed," but God declined. As a result, countless Christians have a deeper understanding of Paul; to them he becomes more human. They see him struggling, living out the principle he gives to us, that God's grace is sufficient.

——————————— **Soul-making** ———————————

Leslie D. Weatherhead, an English author and preacher of this century, struggled with the specific question: "Why doesn't God remove all pain from my life?" To help him understand, he used a human analogy. Think of a physically strong man whose wife often complains because of mysterious ailments. After listening to her, the man gives in and begins helping her walk. After more complaints, he picks her up and carries her wherever she goes. Soon she is an invalid. She cannot take a step; she is totally dependent on him. In this case, it would have been far better for the woman if the man had stood back and watched her stumble, however painfully, to learn to walk on her own.[5] Similarly, by allowing Job to walk on his own in the midst of pain, without the benefit of soothing answers, God let him acquire powerful new strength.

What is God up to with this world? It is clear He does

not intend a hedonistic paradise. But if our happiness is not God's goal, what is? Why does He bother putting up with our world at all?

Some agnostics who can't understand why God allows suffering begin by assuming that man is a fully formed creature who needs a suitable home. Therefore, they demand a pain-free world for mature man to roam. Instead, as Professor John Hick has declared in the book *Philosophy of Religion*, God is dealing with incomplete creatures. Earth's environment should foster the process of "soul-making" in which free beings choose to become children of God. Our world's rough edges allow this process of grappling and confrontation.

We have already seen the advantages of a world which has fixed laws and which allows for human freedom, even though humans can abuse the freedom and harm one another. John Hick takes the Utopian image one step further and claims that a world free of mistakes would actually abort God's designs for us.

Suppose, contrary to fact, that this world were a paradise from which all possibility of pain and suffering were excluded. The consequences would be very far-reaching. For example, no one could ever injure anyone else: the murderer's knife would turn to paper or his bullets to thin air; the bank safe, robbed of a million dollars, would miraculously become filled with another million dollars (without this device, on however large a scale, proving inflationary); fraud, deceit, conspiracy, and treason would somehow always leave the fabric of society undamaged. Again, no one would ever be injured by accident: the mountain-climber, steeplejack, or playing child falling from a height would float unharmed to the ground; the reckless driver would never meet with

*disaster. There would be no need to work; there would
be no call to be concerned for others in time of need or
danger, for in such a world there could be no real needs
or dangers.*

*To make possible this continual series of individual
adjustments, nature would have to work "special prov-
idences" instead of running according to general laws
which men must learn to respect on penalty of pain or
death. The laws of nature would have to be extremely
flexible: sometimes gravity would operate, sometimes
not; sometimes an object would be hard and solid,
sometimes soft. . . .*

*One can at least begin to imagine such a world. It is
evident that our present ethical concepts would have no
meaning in it. If, for example, the notion of harming
someone is an essential element in the concept of wrong
action, in our hedonistic paradise there could be no
wrong actions—nor any right actions in distinction from
wrong. Courage and fortitude would have no point in
an environment in which there is, by definition, no danger of difficulty. Generosity, kindness, the agape aspect
of love, prudence, unselfishness, and all other ethical
notions which presuppose life in a stable environment,
could not even be formed. Consequently, such a world,
however well it might promote pleasure, would be very
ill adapted for the development of the moral qualities
of human personality. In relation to this purpose it would
be the worst of all possible worlds.*

*It would seem, then, that an environment intended to
make possible the growth in free beings of the finest
characteristics of personal life, must have a good deal
in common with our present world. It must operate according to general and dependable laws; and it must*

*involve real dangers, difficulties, problems, obstacles,
and possibilities of pain, failure, sorrow, frustration, and
defeat. If it did not contain the particular trials and perils
which—subtracting man's own very considerable contribution—our world contains it would have to contain
others instead.*

*To realize this is . . . to understand that this world, with
all its "heartaches and the thousand natural shocks
that flesh is heir to," an environment so manifestly not
designed for the maximization of human pleasure
and the minimization of human pain, may be rather
well adapted to the quite different purpose of "soul-
making."*[6]

In a sense, it would be easier for God to step in, to
have faith for us, to help us in extraordinary ways. But
He has chosen to stand before us, loving arms extended,
while He asks *us* to walk, to participate in our own soul-
making. That process involves pain.

C. S. Lewis expands the idea beautifully in *The Problem of Pain*, where he says in part:

> *We want not so much a father in heaven as a
> grandfather in heaven—whose plan for the uni-
> verse was such that it might be said at the end
> of each day, "A good time was had by all."*
>
> *I should very much like to live in a universe
> which was governed on such lines, but since it
> is abundantly clear that I don't, and since I have
> reason to believe nevertheless that God is love,
> I conclude that my conception of love needs
> correction. . . .*
>
> *The problem of reconciling human suffering*

*with the existence of God who loves is only in-
soluble so long as we attach a trivial meaning
to the word "love," and limit His wisdom by
what seems to us to be wise.*

*Over a sketch made idly to amuse a child, an
artist may not take much trouble: he may be
content to let it go even though it is not exactly
as he meant it to be. But over the great picture
of his life—the work which he loves, though in
a different fashion, as intensely as a man loves
a woman or a mother a child—he will take
endless trouble—and would, doubtless, thereby
give endless trouble to the picture if it were
sentient. One can imagine a sentient picture,
after being rubbed and scraped and re-com-
menced for the tenth time, wishing that it were
only a thumb-nail sketch whose making was
over in a minute. In the same way, it is natural
for us to wish that God had designed for us a
less glorious and less arduous destiny; but then
we are wishing not for more but for less.*[7]

Is God trying to tell us something? In a specific way,
responding to a specific throb, it may be dangerous and
perhaps even unscriptural to torture ourselves by looking for His message. The message may simply be that
we live in a world with fixed laws, like everyone else.
But from the larger view, from the view of all history,
yes, God is speaking to us through pain—or, perhaps,
in spite of pain. He can use it to make us aware of Him.
The symphony He is working out includes minor chords,

dissonance, and tiring fugal passages. But those of us who follow His conducting through these early movements will, with renewed strength, someday burst into song.

PART 2

*

How People Respond to Extreme Pain

He can be revealed only to the child; perfectly, to the pure child only. All the discipline of the world is to make men children, that God may be revealed to them.

George MacDonald
Life Essential

* 7 *

Arms Too Short to Box With God

You are lying in a hospital bed, kept alive by tubes of plastic spilling from your arm and nose. Everything you own has been destroyed in a great natural disaster. Your family decimated, no one remains to visit you. All you've worked for—your house, car, savings account—has disappeared forever. You are barely hanging on to life.

You move through the normal stages of questioning, tinged with bitterness. *If only God would visit me personally and give answers,* you say to yourself. *I want to believe Him, but how can I? Everything that's happened contradicts what I know about a loving God. If I could*

*just see Him once and hear Him state His reasons for
putting me through this, I could endure.*

One person, in very similar straits to those described
above, got his wish. Job, the archetypal sufferer, received a personal visit from God, who spoke to him out
of a whirlwind. The reply to Job is the longest single
speech attributed to God in the Bible. Because it is the
Bible's most complete treatise on suffering, it deserves
a close-up look. Perhaps God has already recorded what
He would say directly to us at a time of great suffering.

Reflect on the setting. What could God say to Job?
He might have laid a gentle hand on his head and told
Job how much he would grow in personhood through
the time of trial. He might have revealed His deal with
Satan, emphasizing how important it was for Job to
remain faithful. (He could have given a lecture on the
value of pain, warning Job how much worse his life
would have been if he had Hansen's disease!)

A Nature Lesson

God did none of those things. In a passage that could
be addressed to the Sierra Club or Audubon Society,
God simply reminded Job of all the wonders of nature.
This profound passage is quoted because of its beautiful
poetry, but readers often forget the context in which
Job heard those majestic words: He was homeless,
friendless, naked, ulcerous, in despair. What a time for
a nature-appreciation course!

Before a thoroughly dejected audience, God unleashed unprecedented peals of divine glee. He called
to mind:

—*sunrise.* "Have you ever once commanded the morn-

ing to appear, and caused the dawn to rise in the east?"
—snow. "Have you visited the treasuries of the snow,
or seen where hail is made and stored?"
—thunderstorms. "Who laid out the path for the lightning...? Can you shout to the clouds and make it rain?
Can you make lightning appear and cause it to strike
you as you direct it?"
—a lioness. "Can you stalk prey like a lioness, to satisfy
the young lions' appetites as they lie in their dens, or
lie in wait in the jungle?"
—mountain goats. "Have you ever seen them give birth
to their young?"
—wild donkeys. "Who makes the wild donkeys wild? I
have placed them in the wilderness and given them salt
plains to live in."
—the ostrich. "God has deprived her of wisdom. But
whenever she jumps up to run, she passes the swiftest
horse with its rider."
—the horse. "Have you given the horse strength, or
clothed his neck with a quivering mane? Have you made
him able to leap forward like a locust? His majestic
snorting is something to hear!" (Job 38, 39 LB.)

Stalking lionesses, soaring eagles, streaks of lightning,
crocodiles, wild oxen...God alluded to each with the
delight of a satisfied artist.

After each description, God either stated or implied
to Job, "Are you powerful enough to duplicate these
feats? Are you smart enough to run the world?" He even
employed sarcasm in 38:21: "But of course you know
all this! For you were born before it was all created,
and you are so very experienced!"

God's words hit Job with devastating power. "Stand

up like a man and brace yourself for battle," God demanded. "Let me ask you a question, and give me the answer. Are you going to discredit my justice and condemn me, so that you can say you are right? Are you as strong as God, and can you shout as loudly as he?" (40:7–9.)

Job's response was an overwhelmed, repentant surrender. "I know that you can do anything and that no one can stop you. You ask who it is who has so foolishly denied your providence. It is I. I was talking about things I knew nothing about and did not understand, things far too wonderful for me" (42:2,3).

Does God answer the question of suffering in Job? Not directly. He avoids a logical, point-by-point explanation. Why, then, the accusing tone? What does God want from Job?

Simply an admission of trust. If we, like Job, are so ignorant about the world we live in, a world we can see and touch...who are we to sit in judgment of God's moral government of the universe? Until we are strong enough to make a streak of lightning—or even a gawky ostrich—we have no grounds to sue God. Let him who is about to accuse God consider the greatness of the God accused.

A God wise enough to rule the universe is wise enough to watch over his son Job, *regardless* of how things seem in the bleakest moments. A God wise enough to create me and the world I live in is wise enough to watch out for me.

_____ **Outcries** _____

The attitude which God elicits, and which Job so humbly offers, is strikingly absent from most of the modern books I have read on the problem of suffering. A shelf of all the religious books on this subject would cleanly divide into two groups. The older ones, by Bunyan, Donne, Luther, Calvin, Augustine, and others, are almost embarrassing in their readiness to accept pain and suffering as among God's useful agents. A sense of loyalty and faith in God's wisom undergirds each one. God knows what He is doing in this world, and these authors do not question His actions. They merely try to "justify" the ways of God to man.

More modern books on pain, beginning with some of the agnostic philosophers of the nineteenth century and continuing through to many Christians today, contrast sharply. These authors assume that the amount of evil and suffering in the world cannot be matched with the traditional view of a good and loving God. Therefore, many of them adjust their conception of God, either redefining His love or questioning His power to control evil. If you read these two categories of books side by side, the difference is quite striking. It is as if we in modern times think we have a corner on the suffering market. Do we forget that Luther and Calvin and the others lived in a world without ether and penicillin, and that Bunyan and Donne wrote their greatest works in dungeons?

Suffering from natural causes (in contrast to that caused by man, such as Hitler's imposed suffering) is probaby more controlled now than at any time in history. Why then these outcries against God, these shrieks of despair?

Is our anguished moral indignation completely off-base? God condemned such indignation in Job, accusing him of judging without all the evidence. Could it be that our modern existential angst, our revulsion from suffering, and our questioning of God are futile?

————————— **Response, Not Cause** —————————
It seems to me that suffering involves two main issues: 1) whoever *caused* my discomfort, and 2) my *response*. Most of us expend our energy trying to figure out the cause of our pain before we'll decide how to respond. Joni Eareckson, the subject of chapter 9, consumed two years of exploring possible causes of her accident. But, as Joni found, to the extent that we concentrate on cause, we may well end up embittered against God.

In Job, the portion of the Bible which most vividly poses the question "Who causes pain?" God deliberately sidesteps the issue. He never explained the cause to Job. All the way through, the Bible steers from the issue of cause to the issue of response. Pain and suffering have happened—*now* what will you do? The great discussers of cause, Job's three friends, are dismissed with a scowl. The Bible is so clear on this point that I must conclude the real issue before Christians is not "Is God responsible?" but "How should I react now that this terrible thing has happened?" For that reason, the latter part of this book will be filled with personal examples of people who find different ways of responding to pain.

To the question of the best response, the Bible replies often, with an unsettling answer:

Consider it pure joy, my brothers, whenever you face trials of many kinds, because you know that the testing of your faith develops perseverance. Perseverance

*must finish its work so that you may be mature and
complete, not lacking anything (James 1:2–4 NIV).*

*Dear friends, do not be surprised at the painful trial
you are suffering, as though something strange were
happening to you. But rejoice that you participate in
Christ's sufferings, so that you may be overjoyed when
his glory is revealed (1 Peter 4:12,13 NIV).*

*In this you greatly rejoice, though now for a little
while you may have suffered grief in all kinds of trials.
These have come so that your faith—of greater worth
than gold, which perishes even though refined by
fire—may be proved genuine and may result in
praise, glory and honor when Jesus Christ is revealed
(1 Peter 1:6,7 NIV).*

One of the best examples of the Bible's ideal attitude
toward suffering concerns not physical pain but the
psychological pain which developed after Paul sent a
strongly worded letter to the Christians in Corinth. Reflecting on it, he wrote, "I am no longer sorry that I sent
that letter to you, though I was very sorry for a time,
realizing how painful it would be to you. But it hurt you
only for a little while. Now I am glad I sent it, not because
it hurt you, but because the pain turned you to God. It
was a good kind of sorrow you felt, the kind of sorrow
God wants his people to have, so that I need not come
to you with harshness. For God sometimes uses sorrow
in our lives to help us turn away from sin and seek
eternal life. We should never regret his sending it" (2
Cor. 7:8–11 LB).

"Pain turned you to God"—in my view, this is probably the most accurate, succinct summary of the role

of suffering.* It blends with the Bible's tone of emphasizing the Christian's response, not the cause of the
suffering. It also fits the examples previously cited
where Jesus dealt with two tragedies (Luke 13)—Pilate
butchering Jews and the eighteen men killed by a falling
tower. He followed up each discussion with a ringing
warning, "Don't you realize that you also will perish
unless you leave your evil ways and turn to God?"(v.
3.)

After declaring that these tragedies were not *caused*
by God as a result of men's actions ("Do you think they
were worse sinners than other men from Galilee?"),
He zoomed in on the peoples' *response*. To the non-
Christian, the message is a warning to consider other
values in life and turn to God who offers eternity. To
the Christian, the message is to turn to God in trust, as
a child comes to a parent.

_____ Something Produced _____
How do these suggestions in the Bible differ from the
uncompassionate hospital visitor who brings a smile
and a "Look on the bright side!" pep talk. At first glance
the references sound like a pep talk, especially the

---

*The Bible describes several ways in which suffering can be used for
our good, though I have included all of them under the overall benefit
of "turning us to God."
  For example, suffering can:
  1) Refine our faith (1 Peter, 1:5–7)
  2) Make us mature (James 1:2–4)
  3) Allow an opportunity to display the works of God (John 9:1–3)
  4) Conform us to Christ's image (Rom. 8:28,29)
  5) Produce in us perseverance and character (Rom. 5:3–5)
Martin Luther has an excellent discussion of this topic in his *Treatise
on Good Works*, p. 110, vol. 1 of Tappert's collection of his works.

words "Rejoice!" and "Be glad!" But look closer. Each admonition is followed by a productive result. Suffering *produces* something. It is of value; it changes us. The passages quoted (and alluded to in the footnote on page 88) emphasize different products: rewards, perseverance, patience, character.

This fact, that our response can be a productive response, brings a new understanding to our experience of suffering. We are often willing to undergo productive suffering; athletes and pregnant women volunteer to suffer because of what it will produce. The Bible says that a proper Christian response to suffering gives this same hope to the person on the hospital bed. He can become a better person because of his pain.

The rest of the Bible sheds some light on the words "rejoice" and "be glad." By those words, the apostles did not intend a grin-and-bear-it or act-tough-like-nothing-happened attitude. No trace of those attitudes can be found in Christ's response to suffering, or in Paul's. If those attitudes were the goals, self-sufficiency would be the quickest way to attain them, not trust in God.

Nor is there any masochistic hint of enjoying the pain. "Rejoicing in suffering" does not mean Christians should act happy about tragedy and pain when they feel like crying. Such a view distorts honesty and true expression of feelings. Christianity is not phony.

The Bible's spotlight is on the end result, the use God can make of suffering in our lives. Before He can produce that result, however, He first needs our commitment of trust in Him, and the process of giving Him that commitment can be described as rejoicing.

I asked Dr. Paul Brand to give me examples of Christians he knew who had undergone tremendous suffering. He cited several examples in detail. When I asked whether the pain had turned them toward God or away from God, he thought at length, and concluded that there was no common response. Some grew closer to God, some bitterly drifted from Him. The difference, Brand said, was in their attitude toward cause. Those hung up with questions ("What did I do to deserve this? What is God trying to tell me? Am I being punished?") often bitterly turned against God or else resigned themselves to a fatalistic despair. The most triumphant sufferers were those who sought the best response for Christians and trusted God fully despite their painful conditions.

_____ Mary's Struggle _____

Sometimes the sufferer must undergo months of anguish before learning to turn to God. One of Dr. Brand's most famous patients, Mary Verghese, initially felt grief, bitterness, and agony after a tragic accident.

Mary was not a leprosy patient. Rather, she worked as a resident doctor at Brand's leprosy hospital when he was a missionary in India. One day she went on a picnic outing in a station wagon with other young doctors. The station wagon was driven by a new driver out to demonstrate his bravery. After aggravating moments of driving behind a slow school bus, the young driver jerked the car into the passing lane and floored it. Suddenly he saw another car coming. On his left was a narrow bridge over a culvert. Instinctively he scrambled to stomp on the brake pedal—but hit the gas instead. The station wagon plummeted over the bridge and tum-

*Mary's story is told in *Take My Hands* by Dorothy Clarke Wilson.

bled down a steep embankment.

Mary Verghese, promising young doctor, lay motion-less at the bottom of the bank, her face slit open in a deep gash from cheekbone to chin. Her lower limbs dangled uselessly like two dead tree trunks.

Mary's next few months were almost unbearable. Out-side, the temperature was 110°. In her hospital room, Mary was wrapped in a perspex jacket and a thick plas-tic brace. She faced agonizing hours of therapy. Each week she would fail the sensation tests, never feeling the pinpricks on her legs.

After observing her persistent despair and sourness, Dr. Brand decided to talk to her. "Mary," he began, "I think it's time to begin thinking of your professional future as a doctor." At first she thought he was joking, but he went on to predict that she could serve God as a doctor, perhaps bringing to other patients fresh qual-ities of sympathy and understanding. She pondered his suggestion a long time. She had no idea whether she could ever recover use of her limbs enough to function as a doctor.

Gradually, Mary began to work with the leprosy pa-tients. The staff noticed that patients' self-pity, hope-lessness, and sullenness seemed to fade when Mary Verghese was around. Leprosy patients whispered among themselves about the doctor in a wheelchair who was more disabled than they.

One day, Dr. Brand saw Mary rolling her wheelchair between buildings of the hospital and asked how she was doing. "At first the threads seemed so tangled and broken," she replied, "but I'm beginning to think life may have a pattern after all."

Soon Mary Verghese was assisting at surgery—tedious, exhausting work because she had to maintain her balance and operate while sitting down.

Mary's recovery was to involve many excruciating hours of therapy as well as major spinal surgery. But she had caught a glimmer of hope. She began to see that the disability was not a punishment sent by God to entrap her in a life of misery. Rather, it could be turned into her greatest asset as a doctor. She had instant rapport and acceptance with disabled patients.

Eventually Mary learned to walk with braces. She worked under scholarship in New York's Institute of Physical Medicine and Rehabilitation, and ultimately headed up a new department at the Vellore, India, Physiotherapy School.

By turning toward God and accepting the fact that He could weave a new design for her life, Mary Verghese has probably achieved far more than she ever would have if the accident had not occurred.

In contrast to Mary Verghese, think of the people you know who have turned away from God in time of suffering. Their only alternative is to attract attention to themselves. They talk about their illness as if it's the only part of their lives. They complain, growing shrewish and sullen. They unleash the self-pity that lurks below the surface in each of us. Often, hypochondria inflames their illness. It's as if the only way they can relate to the world is through soliciting pity.

I do not mean to imply that God loves one type of sufferer and rejects the other, or even that one is more "spiritual" than the other. I believe God understands those of us who kick and struggle and scream (two fine examples: the Book of Job and C. S. Lewis' *A Grief Observed*) as well as those few who learn that suffering can be a means of grace to shape them into better persons.

God does not need our good responses for Himself, to satisfy some parental hunger. He focuses attention on our response, I believe, for our sakes, not His. Would it help our condition to know exactly why God is permitting our suffering? Such knowledge may engender even more bitterness. But it does help our condition when God asks us to turn to Him. It can break down our self-sufficiency and create in us a profound new sense of faith in God. And, it can produce changes of lasting value inside us.

_____ **Responding to the Holocaust** _____

Within a two-month period I read two poignant accounts of people who survived the Holocaust of Nazi persecution in World War II. The Holocaust poses the question of God's justice as well as any event in history. How could God let six million of His "chosen people" be savaged? These two authors, Elie Wiesel and Corrie ten Boom, express two radically different responses to the horrible suffering.

Night, by Elie Wiesel, affected me as much as any book I have ever read. In terse, tightly packed sentences, Wiesel describes one of the most horrible chapters of all mankind's history, in which he spent his teen-age years.

Wiesel saw all the Jews in his village banded together in a ghetto, then stripped of their possessions and loaded into cattle cars, where almost a third of them died. He saw his mother, a little sister, and all his family disappear into an oven fueled with human flesh.

Wiesel saw babies pitchforked, children hanged, weak

men killed by fellow prisoners for a piece of bread. Elie himself, frequently battered by the raining blows of truncheons, escaped death only by an accident.

The first night Wiesel's train pulled up at Birkenau, coils of ominous black smoke billowed from a massive oven, and for the first time in his life Elie smelled the scent of burning humans: "Never shall I forget that night, seven times cursed and seven times sealed. Never shall I forget that smoke. Never shall I forget the little faces of the children, whose bodies I saw turned into wreaths of smoke beneath a silent blue sky. Never shall I forget that nocturnal silence which deprived me, for all eternity, of the desire to live. Never shall I forget those moments which murdered my God and my soul and turned my dreams to dust. Never shall I forget these things, even if I am condemned to live as long as God Himself. Never."[1]

All of Wiesel's books drum out an underlying tone of hopeless tragedy. In the foreword to *Night*, French Nobel-prize-winning author Francois Mauriac describes his first meeting with Wiesel, after he had heard his story.

> It was then that I understood what had first drawn me to the young Israeli: that look, as of a Lazarus risen from the dead, yet still a prisoner within the grim confines where he had strayed, stumbling among the shameful corpses. For him, Nietzsche's cry expressed an almost physical reality: God is dead, the God of love, of gentleness, of comfort, the God of Abraham, of Isaac, of Jacob, has vanished forevermore, beneath the gaze of this child, in the smoke of

> *a human holocaust exacted by Race, the most*
> *voracious of all idols. And how many pious Jews*
> *have experienced this death! On that day, hor-*
> *rible even among those days of horror, when*
> *the child watched the hanging (yes!) of another*
> *child, who, he tells us, had the face of a sad*
> *angel, he heard someone behind him groan:*
> *"Where is God? Where is He? Where can He be*
> *now?"*[2]

Tenderly, Mauriac asks, "Have we ever thought about the consequence of a horror that, though less apparent, less striking than the other outrages, is yet the worst of all to those of us who have faith: the death of God in the soul of a child who suddenly discovers absolute evil?"[3]

_____ A Deep Pit _____

There is a tendency for me, and I think many of us, to remain with Wiesel, overwhelmed by human tragedy. After enduring something like Wiesel describes, how can anyone begin living again? Has not the root of all life been severed? Can words like hope, happiness, and joy regain meaning? How can anyone talk about the character-building value of suffering?

Wiesel himself expressed the experience of casting off his humanity as almost a liberating experience. "On the contrary, I felt very strong. I was the accuser, and God the accused. My eyes were open and I was alone— terribly alone in a world without God and without man. Without love or mercy. I had ceased to be anything but ashes, yet I felt myself to be stronger than the Almighty, to whom my life had been tied for so long."[4]

After reading Elie Wiesel's profound account in *Night* and his other books, I read *The Hiding Place*, by Corrie ten Boom. All the pain and suffering of *Night* are present in Corrie's true story of persecution. Corrie was not a Jew, but for aiding Jews she was driven to death camps in Germany. She too saw people murdered, watched her sister die, felt the sting of a whip, and sensed the dissolution of virtue in a world of absolute evil. Though she does not describe the experience with such graphic intensity as Wiesel, she asks many of the same questions and sometimes her anger blazes against God.

But there is another element in *The Hiding Place*, an element which has proved almost untenable to secular reviewers of the subsequent movie—the element of hope and victory. Woven through *The Hiding Place* are threads of small miracles. Bible studies, hymn-sings, acts of compassion and sacrifice. And throughout, Corrie and her sister Betsie continue to trust in a God who sees them and cares.

I must confess that, although my sympathies lie entirely with Corrie's view of life and I believe in her God of love, I had to fight thinking her book shallow compared to Wiesel's. It was as if something dark and sonorous were tugging inside me, pulling me toward despair, urging me to stand proud beside Elie Wiesel as God's accuser by throwing off the confining shackles of belief. I was gripped by the innate human urge to flee to despair, away from hope.

God does not condemn our moments of despair and unbelief. He Himself set the tone by diving into earth and enduring cruel, senseless suffering. Before the final moment, His own Son asked if the cup could pass from Him, and on the cross cried out, "God, why have You forsaken me?" The full range of anger and despair and blackness described so powerfully in *Night* is present in the Christian message—complete identification with the suffering world.

But Christianity takes a further step, which has been a stumbling block to many. It is called the Resurrection, the moment of victory when the last enemy, death itself, was smashed. God, who invites Job and Corrie ten Boom and you and me to step into joy and victory, does not ask us to accept a Pollyannaish world. He simply adds a further, mysterious layer to human experience. He asks for hope in spite of hopeless surroundings. When suffering bleeds us, He asks us not to reject Him, but to respond to Him as children, trusting His wisdom and affirming, as Corrie said, "However deep the pit, God's love is deeper still."

_____ **Dachau Chaplain** _____

At the Protestant Chapel on the grounds of the Dachau concentration camp near Munich, I met with an amazing man who survived the Holocaust and who has taken on a life mission of announcing to the world that God's love is deeper than the sloughs of human depravity. He helped me understand how Corrie's view of life is possible during such a time.

The man, Christian Reger, spent four years as a prisoner in Dachau. His crime? He had belonged to the Confessing Church, the branch of the German state church which opposed Hitler (two of its leaders were Martin Niermoeller and Dietrich Bonhoeffer). Reger was turned over to authorities by his church organist and shipped hundreds of miles away to Dachau.

The International Dachau Committee, of which Reger

is a leader, has worked to restore the camp as a monument so the world cannot forget. "Never Again" is their slogan.

The Dachau camp is difficult to find, since German townsfolk are understandably reluctant to feature it as a tourist mecca. The day I visited it was gray, chill, and overcast. Morning fog still hung low, close to the ground, and as I walked moisture gathered on my face and hands.

Not much of Dachau is left. There are the original cremation ovens, still standing from the war. Thirty barracks existed then, and concrete foundation blocks only a foot high mark out their location. One has been restored, and the visitor is asked to visualize conditions when sometimes 1600 people were pressed into barracks built for a crowded 208.

The fog, the grayness, and the partial buildings added up to an eerie, solemn scene. A child was playing on the foundation blocks of the barracks, and next to the barbed wire fences, lilacs bloomed.

I found Reger in the Protestant Chapel which stands near a Catholic convent and a Jewish memorial. He wanders the grounds, searching out tourists, conversing with them in German, English, and French, answering questions, reminiscing about his inmate days. He tells of the final winter, when coal supplies were low and the ovens were finally shut off. Prisoners no longer had the constant stench of burning comrades hanging over the camp. Then, dead bodies were stacked naked in the snow like cordwood, a number stenciled on each with a blue marker.

Christian Reger will tell the horror stories if you ask. But he will never stop there. He goes on to share his faith—how at Dachau, he was visited by a God who loves.

"Neitzche said a man can undergo torture if he knows the why of his life," Reger told me. "But I, here at Dachau, learned something far greater. I learned to know the Who of my life. He was enough to sustain me then, and is enough to sustain me still."

It was not always so. After his first month in Dachau, Reger had, like Elie Wiesel, abandoned all hope in a loving God. The odds against His existence, from the perspective of a Nazi prisoner, were just too great. Then, in July, 1941, something happened to challenge his doubt. Prisoners were allowed only one letter a month, and exactly one month from the date of his incarceration, Christian Reger received the first news from his wife. The letter, carefully clipped in pieces by censors, chatted about the family and her love for him. At the bottom, was printed a reference to Bible verses: Acts 4:26–29. Reger looked up the verses, part of a speech by Peter and John after being released from prison.

"The kings of the earth take their stand, and the rulers gather together against the Lord and against his anointed One. Indeed Herod and Pontius Pilate met together with the Gentiles and the people of Israel in this city to conspire against your holy servant Jesus, whom you anointed. They did what your power and will had decided beforehand should happen. Now, Lord, consider their threats and enable your servants to speak your word with great boldness" (NIV).

That afternoon Reger was to face interrogators, the most frightening experience in the camp. He would be called on to name fellow Christians, and if he gave in to pressures, those Christians would be captured and possibly killed. There was a good chance he would be beaten with clubs or tortured with electricity if he refused to cooperate with the interrogation. The verses meant little to him. What possible help could God be at a time like this?

Reger moved to the waiting area outside the interrogation room. He was trembling. The door opened, and a fellow minister whom Reger had never met came out. Without looking at Reger or changing the expression on his face, he walked to him, slipped something into Reger's coat pocket, and walked away. Seconds later SS guards appeared and ushered Reger inside the room. The interrogations went well; they were surprisingly easy and involved no violence.

When Reger arrived back at the barracks, he was sweating from tension. He breathed deeply for several moments, trying to calm himself, then crawled into his bunk, covered with straw. Suddenly he remembered the strange incident with the other minister. He reached in his pocket and pulled out a matchbox. *Oh*, he thought, *what a kind gesture. Matches are a priceless commodity in the barracks*. Inside, however, there were no matches, just a folded slip of paper. Reger unfolded the paper, and his heart pounded hard against his chest. Neatly printed on the paper was this reference: Acts 4:26–29.

It was a miracle, a message from God. There was no way that minister could have seen his letter from his wife—he did not even know the minister. God had arranged the event as a demonstration that He was still alive, still able to strengthen, still worthy of trust.

Christian Reger was transformed from that moment. It was a small miracle, as miracles go, but it was enough to found his faith in bedrock that could not be jarred by the atrocities, murders, and human injustice he would see the next four years in Dachau.

"God did not rescue me and make my suffering easier. He simply proved to me that He was still alive, and He still knew I was here. We Christians drew together. We formed a church here, among other convicted pastors and priests—a forced ecumenical movement, we called it. We found our identity as one flesh, as part of Christ's body.

"I can only speak for myself. Others turned from God because of Dachau. Who am I to judge them? I simply know that God met me. For me, He was enough, even at Dachau."

As long as he has health, Christian Reger will stiffly pace the grounds of Dachau, speaking to tourists in his warm, accented voice. He will tell them what it was like and where God was during the long night at Dachau.

_____ **Looking Ahead** _____

Theology offers us a doctrine called Providence to explain this "blue bird on the dung heap" phenomenon. Because of Providence the result of Christian Reger's and Corrie ten Boom's suffering has brought hope and joy to millions. Because of Providence the seeming tragedy of Jesus' crucifixion has become salvation for the world.

Did God desire the Nazi regime or the death of His own Son? Such a question defies answer. Obviously, because of His character He could not desire such atrocities, yet He chose not to prevent them. It helps me to visualize Providence as a forward-looking doctrine. The emphasis I see in the Bible is not to look backward and find out if God is responsible in order to accuse Him. In answering Job, God completely ignored that issue. The emphasis is rather on looking ahead to what God can make of seeming tragedy.

At the instant of pain, it may seem impossible to imagine that good can come. It must have seemed so to Christ at Gethsemane. It is never clear to us how suffering or evil can be transformed into a cause for celebration. But that is what we are asked to believe.

My constant pain oscillates from ridiculously high to excruciating. Why doesn't God answer my prayers?
Brian Sternberg

* 8 *

After the Fall

I
t is all well and good for me to write about the appropriate human response to suffering. But the extent of my present suffering consists of a slight nasal stuffiness—hardly enough to make me an existential witness to the concepts I have laid out. Theories about the role of suffering in the world cannot be worked out apart from real-life experiences.

To learn more, I visited two Christians who daily live out their own lonely battles against pain—physical and psychological—which can rage out of control. Both are young and both were cut down in the prime of life. In many ways, their identity is defined by the misfortune which they met.

Yet the two, Brian Sternberg and Joni Eareckson, have given contrasting human responses. Their experience with suffering has been so consuming that each deserves a full chapter.

On July 2, 1963, Brian Sternberg fell ten feet, and that one-second fall has completely flip-flopped his life. Before the fall the Sternberg family was full of warmth, excitement, fun. In high school Brian had devoted himself to the lofty vision of pole-vaulting. He thrilled to the mad dash down the runway with a pole, the jarring thud when he planted it, the leap with all the recoiled strength of a cougar, the feeling of being slung like a pebble from a slingshot. If you've ever felt a sickening knot in your stomach as you've stood on the edge of a high dive, you have some idea of what Brian Sternberg felt those first tries at the vault.

For Brian it was not enough to excel at vaulting technique. He knew the slight edge some extra grace and skill could give him, so he took up gymnastics.

After high school classes, you could almost always find him practicing vault approaches or perfecting leaps and falls on the trampoline. He learned a wide range of loops and twists and flips, exulting in the sheer pleasure of his body mastery. Gymnastics, a ballet of strength, is perhaps sport's highest claim to art. Brian blended athletic art with the rigorous science of the vault.

As a freshman at the University of Washington, Brian set a national collegiate freshman mark of 15'8". By his sophomore year, he was ranked the No. 1 pole-vaulter in the world by track magazines. He found himself among the world's great athletes. The year was 1963.

John Kennedy was president, and beating the Russians a national pastime. It looked as if the U.S. had a winner in Brian Sternberg, and world attention focused on the nineteen-year-old.

The season of 1963 ushered in unbelievable success. Brian made sports headlines every week. Undefeated in outdoor competition, he set an American record in indoor competition. Then that spring he set his first world mark with a vault of 16'5".

In quick succession Brian racked up new records of 16'7" and 16'8" and captured both the NCAA and AAU titles. Those were great days for the Sternbergs. They knew the glory was short-lived: track stars fade quickly. But it was fun to pile into the family car and see your son single-handedly pack out a fieldhouse and bring the crowd to its feet screaming and waving.

Everything changed on July 2, three weeks after Brian's last world record. Now, well over a decade later, Brian Sternberg still competes, but in a far more lonely and desperate contest. There have been no more vaults.

_____ **The Accident** _____

The ordeal began when he grabbed his sweater and yelled, "I'm going to limber up at the pavilion, mom." He drove across the river to the University of Washington and began a gymnastics warm-up. The U.S. track team was readying for a tour to Russia, and Brian's practice time was now preciously indispensable. This is the way Brian described what happened next:

If there is ever a frightening moment in trampolining, it is just as you leave the trampoline bed, on your way up. At that moment, even the most experienced gymnast sometimes gets a sensation of panic, for no good reason, that does not disappear until he is down safe on the bed again. It hit me as I took off. I got lost in midair and thought I was going to land on my hands and feet, as I had done several times before when the panic came. Instead I landed on my head.

I heard a crack in my neck, then everything was gone. My arms and legs were bounding around in front of my eyes, but I couldn't feel them moving. Even before the bouncing stopped, I was yelling, "I'm paralyzed," in as loud a voice as I could, which was pretty weak because I had practically no lung power. The paralysis was affecting my breathing.

There was nothing I could do. I couldn't move. It scared me at first, but then, for some reason, the panic disappeared. I told the people looking down at me, "Don't move me, especially don't move my neck." At one point, when I started losing my power to breathe and could feel myself passing out, I remember telling a buddy about mouth-to-mouth resuscitation: "Do everything, but don't tilt my head back."

Real anguish hit me a couple of times while we waited for the doctor. It was not physical pain: I just broke from the thought of what had happened to me. But at the time, I was thinking only about the near future. I had not begun to think about the possibility of never walking again.[1]

For the next eight weeks Brian lay strapped onto a Foster frame, a steel-and-canvas device nicknamed "the canvas sandwich." It was hinged at both ends, and every few hours a nurse would flip Brian upside down, preventing bedsores and other complications.

Doctors know little about the spinal system. They

can't study a functioning one without damaging the patient. For forty-eight hours they did not know if Brian would live. When he made it through, they had little idea of what could be restored. Once out of the Foster frame, he could move his head, although for a long time he was afraid to because of his memory of that snapping sound in his neck. He could also twitch a few shoulder muscles, those shrinking bulges that had marked him as a vaulter. Technicians would attach electrodes to other muscles in his body and, by sending voltage through them, cause them to jerk. Otherwise the muscles would deteriorate. Brian could see the twitches, but he felt nothing.

For a while he had no pain. His sensations offered no proof at all that he had legs or arms or a torso. He felt, he said, as if he were floating around the room, for he had no sense of being anywhere. He couldn't even feel the mattress under him.

_____ **Nightmares and an Awakening** _____

While lying in bed all day, a "head" and nothing more, Brian experienced tactile hallucinations. He developed an imaginary pair of legs and arms that he could command at will. He would concentrate hard and think of an object like "basketball." Somehow his subconscious brought to his nerve center the exact memory of a basketball, and it felt just as if he were holding one between his hands. The games were fun at first, because he longed for the day the sensations would hook up with reality.

But then the games turned on him. The objects would stick to his imaginary fingers, and he couldn't let them go. Or he'd feel the sensations of uninvited objects like razor blades. Things with sharp edges would run all over his hands, with excruciating, tearing results. All imaginary, of course, but quite real to Brian's receptors. For a while he couldn't shake the illusion of a nut screwed tightly to each fingertip.

At night came the nightmares. Leering, haunting nightmares of him stomping all over the walls and ceiling of his room, like a fly; others with less shape and plot, just an amorphous feeling of terror. And always after the nightmares came the waking, which was far worse, because he could not awake from the nightmare of reality.

Fits of emotional depression, even more severe than the hallucinations, would come without warning. For hours Brian would look at the same walls and with the same desperate mental lunges try to make his muscles work. He could see his athlete's body shriveling, adapting to his inactivity. And every time he worked hard and failed, he'd dig himself into a deeper hole. He would cry out to the doctors, "I've had it. I don't know what I'm going to do. Nothing's happening; I can't stand lying tied up like this. I'm exhausted. I've tried to move for too long, and I just can't...."[2] The tears and sobs would choke away his speeches.

When the nauseous waves of depression hit, Brian had a few sources of comfort to cling to. One was the support of others—his girl friend and his family. There were also thousands of sympathizers who wrote from as far away as Japan and France and Finland. For an hour or so each day his parents would read them aloud, until they couldn't continue...the emotions were too thick. One seventy-nine-year-old man wrote, "My body's not good, but my spinal cord is fine. I wish I could give it to you."

Support also poured in from the world athletic community. The Russians struck an unprecedented special medal to honor him. Football's Kansas City Chiefs played a benefit game for him.

After weeks the most serious depression set in. Doctors brought no encouragement—no one with Brian's injury had ever walked again. What pulled him out of the hole was a phone conversation with the Fellowship of Christian Athletes conference in Ashland, Oregon. For more than an hour Brian spoke to the athletes and talked with coaches and sports people. These Christians expressed faith for Brian's recovery, and they sparked his own search for faith.

Three months after the accident is the time Brian dates his awakening as a Christian. His brooding had taught him several things. He realized that if he ever walked again it would have to be with God's help. No amount of straining could budge his limbs. If there was dead nerve fiber in his spinal cord, it would have to be remade, and medicine could not do that. Yet he also knew that his faith in God couldn't be a bargain: "You heal me, God, and I'll believe." He had to believe because God was worthy of his faith. He took that risk and committed his life to Jesus Christ.

Brian began a prayer that has not ended. Scores, hundreds, thousands of times he's asked God the same request. Everything about his life reminds him that the prayer has not been answered. He's prayed with bitterness, with pleading, with desperation, with the highest longing. Others have prayed—small clusters of athletes, churches, college students. Always the same prayer, never the answer Brian wants and believes in.

Less than a year after the accident, Brian ended the *Look* magazine article with this quote: "Having faith is a necessary step toward one of two things. Being healed is one of them. Peace of mind, if healing doesn't come, is the other. Either one will suffice." But Brian has a different view now. To him there's only one option—complete healing.

Brian's World

What could feed a faith enough to survive a decade of suffering? Over the years, some who first claimed healing for Brian have changed their prayers. But not the Sternbergs. Were they stubborn or superhuman? I wondered as I drove to their Seattle home. Others had warned me: "It's strange—they just won't accept Brian's condition."

You can't easily set an appointment with Brian. I had to call, speak a message and phone number into a beeping tape recorder, and wait for him to return my call. Brian never knows when he'll feel well enough to see a visitor. The pain, he says, "oscillates from ridiculously high to excruciating."

The Sternberg home perches precariously on the edge of a cliff above Seattle Pacific College. It overlooks a steep street which cars helplessly slide down in severe rain or ice storms. The street was dry, and I made it up okay.

Mrs. Helen Sternberg, Brian's trim, blonde mother, met me at the door. On the roof a friend of Brian's was adjusting a rotating radio antenna. Inside the house, the view of Seattle was spectacular through full-length windows. I watched the traffic for twenty minutes while an orderly prepared Brian.

What strikes a visitor first is how totally Brian depends on other people for his life. If left alone for forty-eight hours, he would die. Orderlies from high schools and Seattle Pacific bathe him, give him medication, feed him, hold glasses of water for him. Brian has always fought against this dependence, but he has no choice. His body lies exactly where the orderly last placed it.

Brian's head is of normal size, but the rest of his body has shrunk due to muscle atrophy. He can now make some motions with his arms. He can hit switches, turn knobs with difficulty, even type with a special contraption that holds back all but one finger.

Brian's room, no larger than an average bedroom, fences in his life. He has no ten-speed bike or skis or ice skates in a garage. He began by showing me the objects around him. An Adidas sports blanket hangs above his bed, a memento of the 1964 Tokyo Olympics Brian never attended. On one wall is a letter from John F. Kennedy, dated August 15, 1963. It was read at the pro football game played for Brian's benefit. Kennedy wrote: "I want you to know that you have been much in our thoughts during these past weeks and that we hope for continued improvement in the days ahead." Brian cried when he heard those words.

He showed the greatest excitement, though, in explaining a complex assortment of ham radio equipment surrounding his bed. With the help of his orderlies he has developed an advanced interest in amateur radio.

He talked slowly and carefully about a variety of subjects. He loves to talk electronics. And he loves to tell stories of his role as an area representative for the

Fellowship of Christian Athletes. He has become a popular speaker for FCA.

FCA officers had told me how Brian, in his wheelchair, has talked as long as an hour to a gym full of athletes, bringing many to tears. Mainly, they see his courage.

_____ **The Miracle That Won't Come** _____

Brian is the first to admit the progress he has made. But now more than ever, he does not accept his condition. He has one hope and one prayer—for total healing. He tells that to every visitor. Medically, he needs a miracle—time has done little, and his chances of natural recovery have steadily diminished.

The worst part is the pain. It's as if Brian's body is in revolt. The pain comes from within and spreads invisibly throughout his whole body, like the pain machine from George Orwell's *1984* that tapped right into the central nervous system. Taken at a single moment, it's enough to knock a strong man howling across the floor. To Brian, it's a horrible routine.

Brian's parents have shared the pain and frustration more than anyone. In the living room they told me of the long struggle of their stricken family. Lights of the city blinked as thousands of commuters snaked their way along the city's streets and bridges. A fire was blazing in the fireplace, and, combined with the view, the setting seemed ideally relaxing. Mrs. Sternberg leaned forward to speak of Brian's dilemma.

After the first shock, which lasted almost six months, the Sternbergs were flooded with genuine expressions of hope and support. Many believed Brian would recover. It had to be God's will, they said, for such a young, talented guy to walk again. Brian has met with famous

Christians known for their healing powers, but he still suffers. At one point, Christian leaders from seven different denominations met in his room, praying and anointing him with oil. Everyone was moved, everyone believed, but nothing happened.

For comfort and guidance the Sternbergs turned to the Bible. They had talked to pastors and theologians of every stripe; they had read all the books on why God allows suffering. As they read, they became even more convinced Brian would be healed.

"What we found," says Mrs. Sternberg, "was that God loves. No, it's more than that. God is love. All around us people were telling us to accept this tragedy as what God must want for us. But the Jesus we saw in the Bible came to bring healing. Where there was hurt, He touched and made well. He never cursed or afflicted people. Jesus was God's language to man. What God is, Jesus lived. Has God's language changed? Does our son's condition contradict what God revealed as Himself?

"People would say to us, 'Well, look at the good that has come of this tragedy. Perhaps God in His wisdom knew Brian would stray away from Him, and so He allowed this to happen.' But the God we found in the New Testament was a God who respected man so much He gave us freedom, even to rebel against Him. The Holy Spirit, we believe, is a gentleman. He suggests and woos, but never forces."

Other Christians who have met extreme suffering have found comfort in learning to accept what is and work from there. Obviously, God doesn't enjoy watching us suffer. But somehow He does permit it. The Sternbergs, though, aren't satisfied with acceptance.

"To put it bluntly," Mrs. Sternberg continues, "I don't think God is very happy with Brian's condition either. God's will as seen in the Bible is a full, abundant life. It's wholeness, health—not the body Brian's trapped in.

"God's will. You can use it as the pious period to every question mark. But God is mysterious and deep. We can never learn too much about Him. We can't stop searching with God and become fatalists, saying, 'I know God's will has been done.' I never read about Jesus saying to a blind man, 'Sorry, buddy, I wish I could help, but God is trying to teach you something, so get used to it.' When Jesus saw a blind man, He healed. And He taught us to pray for God's will to 'be done on earth as it is in heaven.'"

She pauses. The words are strong, and they come with a background of pain few others have felt.

She presses her chin in her hands. "In this life, we don't know the full answers to any questions. We take a lot on faith. My husband and I and Brian cling most strongly to God's love. If something—like the accident—doesn't tally with God's love, we look elsewhere. We know it's not from Him.

"I don't know why Brian's not on his feet yet. I believe God is all-powerful, but I also believe He's limited Himself. Satan is strong. And I think it's to Satan's great advantage to keep us incapacitated. Anything to keep us from wholeness. He'll exploit our weakness, like a boxer jabbing again and again at a sore jaw or bloody eye. He doesn't quit."

As she talked of the battle between good and evil, I thought of Satan's attacks on Jesus while He was on earth—a slaughter of babies, temptations, betrayal, and finally death. Good Friday must have seemed victorious from Satan's viewpoint. Yet God transformed the awful, grisly death of His own Son into His greatest victory.

In smaller, more subtle ways He has used Brian's tragedy, too—bringing Brian Sternberg and hundreds more to Himself. Yet will He crash through with a resounding turn of the tables, wiping out the tragedy with a healing as He had wiped out death with a resurrection? The Sternbergs are staking everything on this hope.

Mrs. Sternberg continues, "No one in Brian's condition has ever walked. No one. Yet we still believe. I have no idea when God will heal Brian. It's conceivable this particular battle will not be won here on earth. Some people you pray for are healed. Some aren't in this world. But that doesn't change God's desire for wholeness—body, mind, and spirit.

"We won't give up. We're like doctors searching for a cure; we won't stop investigating. We think it pleases God for us to persevere."

_____ **Two Images** _____

The years since 1963 have not been all despair. The line of paralysis on Brian's chest has crept down, sometimes as much as three-eighths of an inch a year. And another miracle of sorts has occurred. Through a decade and a half of fatigue and tension, neither Mr. nor Mrs. Sternberg has ever been ill.

The Sternbergs found one concept that gives them strength—a definition of disease: Where there is disease between me and God, between me and myself, or between me and a fellow-man, this is disease, and it calls for healing!

For two-and-one-half years the Sternbergs prayed for a healing ministry that would encompass their broad-

ened definition of disease. Finally one came into being:
a monthly, Sunday-night prayer service in a Seattle
church. People with hurts and needs attend. Those who
want to come forward, spend a few silent minutes with
the pastor, while all the rest direct their prayers to the
one person's needs. The results have been beautiful,
and the church has come together remarkably. The
practice has spread far beyond Seattle.

Some would see results like that as the reason for
the tragic injury. To the Sternbergs this is no justifi-
cation. "We believe in a loving God," they say. "Loving
in the way Jesus showed. And we intend to show that
to the world."

It was late, and our conversation had to end. Before
I left the Sternberg house, though, I asked to see Brian's
sports mementos. We went into a separate room
crowded with massive trophies, plaques, and certifi-
cates. One named him 1963's outstanding athlete of the
continent.

A photo on one wall caught my eye. It showed him
breaking his last world record at Compton, California.
He was sailing horizontally over the bar, his arms
straight ahead, every muscle in his body rippling and
tense. The action was frozen by electronic flash, and in
a way it's been frozen ever since. I felt a wash of pain
and sorrow—the body I had met and talked with was
a pitiful shadow of this superb body. Brian has grown,
of course, emotionally, spiritually. But he has shrunk,
too. Pain wears. It has consumed more than a decade
of his life. Brian is almost thirty-five now.

I couldn't get the two images out of my mind as I
stepped out of the warmth into a chilly Seattle wind.
The Brian of the photo. And Brian today—the twisted,

helpless body, lying on his bed where he'll be tomorrow, the next day...who knows how long?

Could I believe if that were me? Would I rationalize or accept or rebel? And if I could believe, would belief survive thirteen, fourteen, fifteen years? Were the Sternbergs right in gambling everything on a miracle that has not come despite thousands of prayers? Were they unfairly dictating terms to God? Should they accept and "praise the Lord anyhow" as some would suggest?

I don't know. What stood out strongest was the fierce, fighting quality of their faith.

As I drove away, what struck me was not pity for Brian. It was a thick, lumpy realization that I had met strength. Strength that would endure, even if the specifics never fell into line.

An analogy used by Paul Tournier came to mind as I started the jerky, braking descent of the Sternbergs' street. He said the Christian life is sometimes like a trapeze act. You can swing on the bar, exercising and building muscles all you want. But if you want to excel, you have to let go, with nothing beneath you, and reach out for the next trapeze bar. Brian would have liked that analogy, I thought. He knew what it means to let go.

A long time ago the Sternbergs together let go of the props and told the world they would believe God, despite...anything. Brian sees that as his calling. Not as many spectators are standing around watching now, but the Sternbergs still believe. I drove away, stirred by their tenacious belief.

My need for help is obvious every day when I wake up, flat on my back, waiting for someone to come dress me. I can't even comb my hair or blow my nose alone!

Joni Eareckson

* 9 *

On My Feet Dancing

Anumber of months passed between my visits to Brian Sternberg and to Joni Eareckson.* Having heard bits and pieces of her story, I anticipated the same mood I had found at the Sternbergs: an uncompleted, uncomfortable struggle mixed with tough, undying faith. What more could be expected from a young person left with a body that did not work? But the mood at Joni's house, completely cross-country from Brian's, was quite different.

*Joni's complete story is told in the book *Joni* by Joni Eareckson with Joe Musser, Zondervan © 1976.

You reach Joni Eareckson's home by following one of the creeks west of Baltimore which swelled to a torrent when Hurricane Agnes swept through several years ago. The stream is tranquil now, and beautiful.

The road slithers through S-turns around abrupt, lumpy hills. You are surrounded by hardwood forest until you reach the crest of the highest hill, where a sweeping panoramic landscape suddenly unfolds. Joni's house is on that hill. It's a cottage made of large boulders and hand-hewn timber, painstakingly fitted together by Joni's father. A massive barn looms just in front of the cottage: it, too, is handmade with a huge rock foundation and unstained wood.

Joni's studio juts out over the hill, its glass walls allowing a perfect view. A brown stallion is usually grazing in the valley, swishing his tail at flies. A Great Dane romps through the grass.

Many artists live tucked away in rustic settings like this one. But Joni's life is different from theirs. She never leaves her studio unless someone pushes her. And she draws with a pen held between her teeth. She has to— she's paralyzed. Her hands are limp and useless.

Joni used to visit the cottage as a teen-ager. Then she rode her stallion through forest trails at breakneck speed, splashed in the creek with the Great Dane, and slapped basketballs against a backboard beside the cottage. Sometimes she would even join a fox hunt through the property.

But now Joni's daily exercise consists of minute movements. She can move her arm with a biceps-and-shoulder motion. So, by hooking a fork into a metal slot on her hand brace, she can feed herself. And by keeping her fingernails long, she can turn the pages of a book.

Most of her day, though, is taken up with the movements of drawing—meticulous, subtle nods and slides of her head as she bites down on a pen with her teeth. Slowly, a recognizable scene takes form.

A decade has passed since the accident, a two-second mistake that completely changed Joni's life. Yet her buoyant optimism has not changed. Her face is alive, her eyes bright and expressive. Her spirit is so effervescent that she faintly brings to mind all those "Think positive—love yourself!" courses taught by former Miss Americas. Unlike them, however, Joni's spirit was squeezed out of tragedy.

A Fateful Dive

Summer had been especially hot and humid that year, 1967. July was stifling. I practiced with the horses in the morning, working up a sweat that only a dip in the bay could cool. My sister Kathy and I rode to the Chesapeake Bay beach and dove into the murky water.

I was never content to swim laps in a pool or splash around in the shallow part of the bay. I liked free swimming, in the open water. A raft floating fifty or sixty yards offshore was a perfect target, and Kathy and I raced to it. We were both athletic, and sometimes reckless.

When I reached the raft, I climbed on it and quickly dove off the side. It was a fast motion, done almost without thinking. I felt the pull of the water . . . and then a stunning jolt . . . my head crashed into a rock on the bottom. My limbs splayed out. I felt a loud buzzing, like an electric shock accompanied by intense vibration. Yet there was no pain.

I couldn't move! My face was pressing against the

grinding sand on the bottom, but I couldn't get up. My mind was directing my muscles to swim, but nothing responded. I held my breath, prayed, and waited, suspended face-down in the water.

After maybe a minute I heard Kathy calling me—a faint, muffled voice above the water surface. Her voice came closer and clearer, and then I saw her shadow right near me. "Did you dive in here? It's so shallow," I heard her say.

Kathy reached down, tried to lift me, then stumbled. Oh, God. How much longer, I thought. Everything was going black.

Just as I was about to faint, my head broke through the surface and I choked in a great gulp of air. I tried to hold on to Kathy, but again my muscles would not respond. She draped me over her shoulders and began paddling to shore. Sure that my hands and legs were tied together around my chest, with a sudden shock of horror I realized that my limbs were dangling motionless over her shoulder.

I had lost touch with my body.

An ambulance rushed Joni from the solitude of the bay to a whirl of activity at Baltimore's City Hospital. She was put in a small room blocked off by privacy curtains. One nurse asked about her medical history. Another clipped off her brand-new swimming suit, leaving her exposed and feeling even more helpless. A doctor came by with a long metal pin and kept asking, "Do you feel this?" as he pressed it against her feet, her calves, her fingers, and her arms. Concentrating as hard as she could, Joni responded only when he tested her shoulders.

After some hurried consultation with other doctors,

one named Dr. Sherrill chopped off Joni's flowing blonde hair with electric clippers, and a nurse shaved her head. Then she heard the high, whining sound of an electric drill. She began fading from consciousness, her last memory of someone holding her head while the doctor drilled two neat holes, one on either side of her skull.

_____ **The Mirror** _____

When Joni awoke, she found herself strapped into a Stryker frame (similar to Brian Sternberg's Foster frame). Her face poked through a small opening in the canvas sheet to which she was trapped. Every two hours a nurse would flip the frame. Two views: the floor and the ceiling.

Metal tongs, like ice tongs, were inserted into the holes in her head and attached to a spring device which pulled her head away from her body.

Despite the lack of mobility and the depressing atmosphere of the Intensive Care Unit, Joni survived the first few weeks in good spirits. The pain was slight, and doctors hoped some of the nerves would repair themselves. In those early days her room was crowded with visitors and flowers and gifts. Her two sisters would spread out *Seventeen* magazines on the floor for her to read.

After four weeks, when Joni had passed the critical stage, Dr. Sherrill performed a fusion operation on her spinal cord. At first, Joni was exultant, utterly convinced the surgery would solve her problems and put her on her feet again. The surgery was successful, but that same day Dr. Sherrill leveled with her. "Joni," he said, "I'm sorry, but the injury is permanent. Fusion surgery

didn't change that. You'll never walk again. You arms
will have limited use."

For the first time since the accident, that fact sunk
in. She had expected a few more months' treatment,
then rehabilitation, then recovery. Suddenly she saw
that her whole life style would change. No more sports
cars, horse shows, lacrosse matches. Maybe no more
dates. Ever.

"I was devastated," she recalls. "My life had been so
full. I had been involved in as many school activities as
I could squeeze in. And suddenly I found myself all
alone, just a bare, immobile body between two sheets.
My hobbies and possessions were meaningless to me.
Those beautiful horses in the barn which I used to trick-
ride, standing on their shoulders—I could never ride
them again. I couldn't even feed myself. I could sleep
and breathe; everything else was done for me."

Strapped to the canvas facing downward, Joni
watched hot, salty tears fall from her face and drip
designs onto the floor. Her nose ran, and she had to
call for a nurse. She even needed help to cry.

Joni's spirits fell to greater depths a few days later.
Two friends from school visited her for the first time.
Their last image of Joni had been the vivacious, ener-
getic athlete, so they were totally unprepared for what
weeks in the hospital had done. They came to Joni's
bedside, and their mouths dropped. "Oh, my God," whispered one of the girls. Shocked, they stood in awkward
silence, then ran outside. Joni could hear one girl vom-
iting and one girl sobbing outside her hospital door.
She wondered what could be so horrible to cause such
a reaction.

A few days later, she found out. Joni asked a visitor,

Jackie, for a mirror. Jackie stalled, but Joni insisted. Nervously, Jackie brought her one. Joni took one look in the glass and screamed, "Oh, God, how can You do this to me!"

The person in the mirror had bloodshot eyes, sunken in dark cavities far back into her skull. Skin color had faded to a dull yellow. Her teeth were black from medication. Her head was still shaved, with metal clamps on either side. And her weight had shrunk from 125 to 80 pounds.

Joni sobbed and wailed. "Oh, Jackie, I need your help. Please do one thing for me. I can't face it any longer."

"What's that, Joni?' I'll do anything for you."

"Help me die, Jackie. Bring me some pills, or a razor blade even. I can't live inside a grotesque body like this. Help me die, Jackie."

Jackie could not bring herself to obey, regardless of Joni's condition. So Joni learned another cruel fact: she was too helpless to die on her own.

_____ Fullness _____

Thousands of people have met Joni since that awful day in City Hospital. She has been a popular speaker at banquets, camps, youth groups, and large conventions. She's been featured on NBC's "Today" show and in magazines like *People*. Her artwork graces cards, posters, and stationery in shops around the country. Almost everyone who meets her comes away feeling happier, more hopeful. She is miles away from the shriveled, pitiable girl in the mirror.

It is a part of the lonely burden of handicapped people that the simple act of living—keeping house, eating, getting dressed—require enormous effort. Joni has pushed beyond those routine actions and now supports herself through sales of art work and her own bookstore. How has she done it?

"Once, during those depressing days in the hospital when my day consisted of pancake flips to ease the bedsores, a visitor tried to cheer me up," Joni remembers. "He quoted a Bible verse to me, a promise which Jesus left His followers: "I have come to give you life in all its fullness."

"I was so bitter and cynical then, the thought was almost a mockery. Life in all its fullness? If I struggled the rest of my life, the most I could foresee would be a half-life, or some pitied, inferior form of life. No more tennis, no making love, or marriage . . . no real contribution.

"In the last ten years, my outlook has changed. I awake every day, grateful for what God has given me. Somehow—and it took me three years to admit it— God has proven to me that I, too, can have a fullness of life."

Joni's first lesson was the first lesson of any handicapped person—to accept her condition with its limitations. It was futile to close her eyes and moan about her awful physical condition. Wishing would not change the face in the mirror. She had to accept herself as a quadriplegic and find new ways of coping.

The process was painful. When Joni's boyfriend would put his arm around her and squeeze her, she did not feel it. She kept fighting a temptation to fantasize. She would spend hours with her eyes shut, imagining what it would be like if she were well again. She would have a fiance, drive a sports car, take long hikes in the woods, star on a college lacrosse team . . . the possibilities were endless. But they were also worthless, and Joni soon learned that dwelling on them did not relieve her. They only delayed her self-acceptance.

Joni quickly learned that "normal" people are very uncomfortable around the handicapped. In talking to her, some people would speak loudly and enunciate clearly, using simple words, assuming she was mentally deficient. On a sidewalk, as someone pushed her in a wheelchair, pedestrians would allow a five-foot berth, stepping off the curb to let her by, though the sidewalk was wide enough for both to pass. Joni learned why some handicapped people in the hospital showed no desire to leave for the outside world. Inside, *they* were the normal people. Everyone had braces or splints or traction or gauze bandages in the hospital. And professionals were trained to care for them and understand.

Friends helped. Joni's most thrilling memory of those days came about a year after her injury. In a crazy moment, a friend raced her wheelchair across a sand beach and pushed her into the pounding Atlantic surf. Joni squealed with delight. She would never be able to body-surf on the rolling waves again, but she could at least feel the lapping tide and the salt spray against her cheeks. She loved it when people treated her in that carefree way, instead of always being delicate and cautious around her.

But even the ability to sit in a wheelchair was preceded by months of agonizing therapy. After lying horizontal for months, Joni had to be gradually raised to a vertical, sitting position. The first time a nurse raised her even to a 45-degree angle, she nearly collapsed from nausea and dizziness as her heart tried to adjust to the new demands.

Ugly bedsores kept developing. Around her tailbone and hips, sharp edges of bone would protrude through skin. To alleviate the pressures, doctors operated (with Joni fully conscious—she felt no pain and needed no anesthesia) and filed away the sharp bones in her hips and tailbone. More weeks in bed followed, then a repeat of the grueling exercises of sitting up. Sometimes the skin would break around the bones again, and she would have to undergo further surgery.

In these times, Joni leaned heavily on friends for emotional support. A cluster group of Christian students would visit her faithfully. Once they surprised her by smuggling a puppy into her hospital room. Joni giggled as the puppy slathered her face with his tongue.

────────────── **Forty-Year Delay** ──────────────

At first, Joni found her condition impossible to reconcile with her faith in a loving God. It seemed all God's gifts, the good things she had enjoyed as an active teen-ager, had been stolen from her. What did she have left?

The turning to God was slow. Change from bitterness to trust in Him dragged out over three years of tears and violent questionings.

One night especially, Joni became convinced that God did understand. Pain was streaking through her back in a way that is a unique torment to those paralyzed. Healthy persons can scratch an itch, squeeze an aching muscle, or flex a cramped foot. The paralyzed must lie still, defenseless, and feel the pain.

Cindy, one of Joni's closest friends, was beside her bed, searching desperately for some way to encourage Joni. Finally, she clumsily blurted out, "Joni, Jesus knows how you feel—you aren't the only one—why, He was paralyzed too."

Joni glared at her. "What? What are you talking about?"

Cindy continued, "It's true. Remember He was nailed on a cross. His back was raw from beatings, and He must have yearned for a way to move to change positions, or redistribute His weight. But He couldn't. He was paralyzed by the nails."

The thought intrigued Joni. It had never occurred to her before that God had felt the exact piercing sensations that racked her body. The idea was profoundly comforting.

God became incredibly close to me. I had seen what a difference the love shown me by friends and family had made. I began to realize that, yes, God also loved me.

Few of us have the luxury—it took me forever to think of it as that—to come to ground zero with God. Before the accident, my questions had always been, "How will God fit into this situation? How will He affect my dating life? My career plans? The things I enjoy?" All those options were gone. It was me, just a helpless body, and God.

I had no other identity but God, and gradually He became enough. I became overwhelmed with the phenomenon of the personal God, who created the universe, living in my life. He would make me attractive and worthwhile—I could not do it without Him.

The first months, even years, I was consumed with the unanswered questions of what God was trying to teach me. I probably secretly hoped that by figuring out God's ideas, I could learn my lesson and then He would heal me.

I guess every Christian with an experience similar to mine goes back to the Book of Job for answers. Here was a righteous man who suffered more than I could imagine. Everything was taken away from him. Strangely, the Book of Job does not answer any questions about why God let the tragedies happen. But Job clung to God, and God rewarded him.

"Is that what God wants?" I wondered. My focus changed from demanding an explanation from God to humbly depending on Him.

Okay, I am paralyzed. It's terrible. I don't like it. But can God still use me, paralyzed? Can I, paralyzed, still worship God and love Him? He has taught me that I can.

Maybe God's gift to me is my dependence on Him. I will never reach the place where I'm self-sufficient, where God is crowded out of my life. I'm aware of His grace to me every moment. My need for help is obvious every day when I wake up, flat on my back, waiting for someone to come dress me. I can't even comb my hair or blow my nose alone!

But I have friends who care. I have the beauty of the scenery. With my art sales, I can even support myself financially—the dream of a handicapped person.

The peace that counts is an internal peace, and God has lavished me with that peace.

And there's one more thing. I have hope for the future. The Bible speaks of our bodies being "glorified" in heaven. In high school that was always a hazy, foreign concept. But now I realize that I will be healed. I haven't been cheated out of being a complete person—I'm just

*going through a forty-year delay, and God is with me
even through that.*

*Being "glorified"—I know the meaning of that now.
It's the time, after my death here, when I'll be on my
feet dancing.*

_____ **The New Barn** _____

After two years of rehabilitation, Joni could maneuver
a motorized wheelchair well enough to drag-race down
hospital hallways. She enrolled in a college speech
course and eventually became a speaker much in demand.

Joni captivates an audience. She is immaculately
dressed, and every blonde hair is neatly in place. As
she speaks, she retraces the events of the accident and
her long recovery. Her words flow articulately.

Audiences most appreciate Joni's zest for life and her
enthusiasm. Her limbs stay motionless, but her eyes
and face sparkle with expression. She describes the
cottage and the beautiful scenery surrounding her studio. "Though I can't splash in the creek and ride the
horses," she says, "I can sit outside, and my senses are
flooded with smells and textures and beautiful sights."
She reproduces those scenes, sometimes before an audience, with the incredible process of mouth-artistry.

In her talks, Joni often refers to the massive barn just
outside her studio. It's Joni's favorite building on the
farm. Inside are housed her fondest memories: the
sweet-smelling hay, the rustling sounds of restless
horses, and the dark corners she played in as a child.

Joni describes its enchantment, its beauty, and her
father's pride in its workmanship. But then she describes a horrible memory: a fire set by vandals which

utterly destroyed the barn. That terrifying scene is etched in her mind: the wild screams of her pet horses, the smell of burning flesh, the frantic efforts of her family and neighbors to contain the fire.

The story does not end there, however. Her father, stooped and twisted from arthritis, began again the arduous task of reconstructing the barn. The foundation remained, and on top of it he fitted new boulders, new beams, and new boards. The second barn, the re-created one, is every bit as grand as the first.

"I am like that barn," Joni says. "I thought my life had been crushed out. But, with the help of God and my friends, it has been rebuilt. Now can you understand why I'm so happy? I've recovered what I thought would always escape me—life in all its fullness."

_____ **Two Who Suffer** _____

Joni Eareckson and Brian Sternberg stand for those unfortunate persons for whom pain seems to be in revolt. Paralyzed limbs, bodies wracked with cancer, thumping migraine headaches—those are ailments whose bearers would undoubtedly cringe from a concept like "the gift of pain." To them, the phrase must sound hollow and sadistic; pain has left its natural cycle and become a Frankenstein.

Yet it impressed me that Brian and Joni have each found a unique way of continuing, and their trust in God is an integral part of that survival process.

Brian squarely faces the question of causation. Is God responsible? He and his parents are convinced that his condition is as abhorrent to God as it is to them. His conclusions run counter to some themes in this book, for he disallows such thoughts as the value given by his unique suffering. Though recognizing that God has providentially used his pain to bring good, he blasts the concept that God could allow such a condition for the rest of his life. He has gambled his faith, and almost his theology, on the hope for healing.

Yet, even that position, which seems more and more insupportable to the Sternbergs' friends, is a definite turning to God. Brian has learned to trust and believe in a loving, worthy God despite torment which few will ever experience. In heaven, Brian will surely walk with the confident stride of a Job or Habakkuk or Corrie ten Boom, who saw the world at its worst and still believed.

Brian epitomizes one quality which every suffering person can learn from. His fierce, fighting faith sustains him. To him, it is faith in a miracle. To others, it may be faith in rehabilitation or in God's ability to use them despite the pain.

Joni Eareckson's pain, except for brief flashes, has been mostly psychological. Yet many who have heard her speak have been ashamed of their own feelings of discontent. Her life is marked with a prevailing grace note of triumph and joy. After prolonged wrestling with God, she turned to Him and He gave her a depth which shocks mature Christians.

Thank God, very few of us will endure the trials of Joni or Brian. They bring an unusual experiential body to the skeleton of faith. However their lives fit into such schemes as "the gift of pain," at least they have not been crushed by massive suffering. No matter how deep the pit, God's love is deeper still. Their continuing faith makes my own pains easier to bear.

I think of Jesus' profound, triumphant statement in John 16:33: "In this world you will have trouble. But take heart! I HAVE OVERCOME THE WORLD" (NIV), He declared with serene finality. I can imagine the chill bumps on the backs of the eleven men who heard that assertion from the lips of God in flesh.

Yet, hours later, all eleven had lost faith in those words. The God-man who spoke then had somehow been beaten by death itself. For a few days, it surely appeared as though the world had overcome God.

The mystery of suffering is a Christian paradox. Pain jostles with triumph and rubs elbows with despair. And yet, people like Joni and Brian show us that Christians in the worst prison of suffering can still hear and believe Christ's words: I HAVE OVERCOME THE WORLD.

What doesn't destroy me makes me stronger.
                                                    John Perkins

* 10 *

Other
Witnesses

Because of my writing career, I have visited a number of Christian leaders, the "stars" who speak at large conferences and whose pictures are often seen in religious magazines. Some are athletes or performers who are spotlighted because they happen to be Christian. Others are unknowns who have a good dose of Christian wisdom. But of all these people I've talked with, I think back most gratefully to one unlikely man in rural Mississippi, near the town of Mendenhall...a man who is etched in a special place in my mind. When I left Mr. Buckley's house, I felt I had left the presence of a saint.

Once a group of white college students, fascinated by Mr. Buckley's tales of the Old South, came with a cassette recorder to interview him. He talked for three-and-a-half hours. Then he paused for a glass of water, took a good long sip, swished it around in his mouth, and announced, "Well, that brings us up to 1901." Mr. Buckley is almost ninety.

Mr. Buckley's house was the nicest black home I visited in Simpson County, Mississippi. It is brick on the outside, wood-paneled on the inside, and includes four or five large rooms. Most days, though, Mr. Buckley spends sitting in a wooden rocker by the kitchen fireplace, the way he used to sit around Home Comfort stoves in the one-room shacks of rural Mississippi. That's where he was when I saw him—rocking, reminiscing, scratching his close-cropped gray hair, and chuckling over how life used to be. His skin was thick and leathery, burnt that way by decades of Mississippi sun.

Flies danced around the room, Mrs. Buckley tended her pot of black-eyed peas on the stove, and occasionally Mr. Buckley would clear his throat and spit in the fireplace. He had good aim.

He was born just twenty-five years after slavery was abolished, and he survived Southern anger and bitterness after Reconstruction. He lived in Mississippi through the fearful, early days of the Ku Klux Klan, listening to their threats, watching crosses burn, hearing rumors of lynchings and burnings. And after twenty-five years of being banned from white restaurants, white motels, white bathrooms, and white polling booths, Mr. Buckley joined the Civil Rights movement in the mid-

sixties. Believing God could use him, he began working
for Rev. John Perkins in voter registration.*

_____ **Leading the Movement** _____

At that time, no one in Simpson County would rent a
building to the federal marshals who came to register
the blacks. The black people had no spare buildings;
the whites wouldn't think of letting theirs be used. Finally the marshals set up registration lines inside a wire
fence around the rear loading docks of the post office.
In a county with over 5,000 black adults, only 50 were
registered to vote then.

Buckley helped to organize buses and vans to bring
blacks to the post office. Each name on voter lists was
carved out in fear. Some blacks who registered lost their
jobs. A hostile crowd of whites would sometimes appear, shouting insults, threatening. But the blacks came.
Strong black men, bowed from carrying cotton sacks
on their backs, formed a courageous line through down-
town Mendenhall to ask for their vote. Eventually 2,300
were registered.

Through his years as a leader in the black community
near Mendenhall, Mr. Buckley has walked with God, and
the lashes and wounds he has suffered for it have made
him a deeper, stronger man. His strength in the face of
a system that has broken strong men made me think
of Jesus' words, "Blessed are the poor." Most of the
poor I saw in Mississippi didn't seem very blessed. Mr.
Buckley, though, demonstrated how the poor and the
oppressed could be blessed. His faith in God was all he

_____

*The complete story of John Perkins' work in Mississippi is told in
Let Justice Roll Down, © 1976, Gospel Light Publishers.

had when days were dark and nights were filled with sleepless fear. He grasped his faith and lived with it as an old friend. And now God resides in him with a visible ease and familiarity.

Mr. Buckley's faith was tested most severely during a period in December, 1969, when Rev. John Perkins' local radio ministry was practically shut down by an ugly incident of racial violence. Later that month, the Buckleys were asleep in their new home, still scented with paint, when Mr. Buckley suddenly awoke at two o'clock in the morning. He smelled smoke and jumped out of bed just in time: the hallway of their house was blazing, and flames were creeping along the baseboard to their bedroom. He and his wife escaped, barely, but lost all their possessions. The fire had been set by their neighbors.

Mr. Buckley says, "Well, I reckon we been through a lot. I lost two of my three children, and I lost my first wife, and we almost got ourselves killed that night, fo' sure. But the Lord say He won't put more on us than we can stand. If we can't take it, He'll be right there beside us giving stren'th we didn't know we had."

Right now, Mr. Buckley's dream is to make a tiny church in Mendenhall an example of the New Testament church, where people who pray expect answers, and where people are known by their love for one another. He talked at length about his desire to see the congregation grow.

_____ **Not Destroyed** _____

"What doesn't destroy me makes me stronger," John Perkins had said to me while describing his and Buckley's struggles in Mississippi. Mr. Buckley's peaceful, wrinkled face seemed to prove it. Like a tough old oak which has weathered thunderstorms and blizzards, Mr. Buckley exudes a quality of strength that most of us sheltered Americans will never experience. There's something unique about having only God to lean on in times of trial.

After the hours I spent with Mr. Buckley, I finally understood Jesus' strange, paradoxical words in the Beatitudes. I had always viewed Jesus' words "Blessed are the poor," etc. as a sop Jesus threw to the unfortunates, like a pat on the back. But meeting poor blacks in Mississippi changed my mind. Mr. Buckley *was* blessed, with a quality of life that I had not met in any other person, including all the Christian "stars." His faith was solid, aged, and worn.

The apostle Paul uses a strange phrase, "His [God's] strength is made perfect in weakness." It is a phrase misunderstood and perhaps ridiculed by those who blast God for allowing pain and suffering in this world. We expect the poor and suffering to rebel. But in examples like Paul and Mr. Buckley, the phrase rings loudly with truth. There is a sense in which pain firms us, adds extra layers. Even of Jesus it was said, "He learned obedience from what he suffered" (Heb. 5:8 NIV).

It is no accident that some of the most inspiring stories of faith come from those often considered "losers" by the rest of the world. Hesitantly, C. S. Lewis concludes: "I am not convinced that suffering . . . has any natural tendency to produce such evils (anger and cynicism). I did not find the front-line trenches of the C.C.S. more full of hatred, selfishness, rebellion, and dishonesty than any other place. I have seen great beauty of spirit in some who were great sufferers. I have seen men, for the most part, grow better not worse with advancing years, and I have seen the last illness produce treasures of fortitude and meekness from most unpromising subjects.... If the world is indeed a 'vale of soul-making,' it seems on the whole to be doing its work."[1]

_____ **Leo's Legacy** _____

It is difficult, and certainly presumptuous, for one not undergoing acute suffering to write on the benefits it produces. Possibly the only way to discuss the point is through repeated illustrations of human experience. Thousands of people who have seen the film *Leo Beuerman* know yet another example of God's beauty being worked out through human weakness.

Leo Beuerman is a unique human, a genetic freak. His body is shriveled, twisted, dwarfed, and all his features are disproportionate. Though he is fully adult in the film (in his sixties), he is less than two feet tall. Throughout his life, wherever Leo went, people looked quickly away from him. Yet he did not spend his life in bed or in a home for the handicapped. He lived on an Iowa farm with his mother, doing the respectable (but agonizing for him) trade of watch repair. After his sheltering mother died, Leo ventured farther into the outside world. He made a tiny red cart. Every day meant a ritual for him, a painful and time-consuming hoisting his cart onto a specially designed tractor. His hands moved awkwardly, never quite in the direction he intended. Screwing on a bolt was a tedious chore involving several tries.

But pain could be ignored. And Leo's time had to be filled somehow. So each day he made the pilgrimage on his tractor to town. There, he carefully lowered himself and his cart down the complex ladder of chains and hoists.

After that, Leo was ready for business. He patiently waited in his cart, his wares—watches, pencils, and pens—spread out before him. His customers were mostly children and those who chose to disregard his grotesque and deformed features.

"I guarantee it," a hand-lettered sign on Leo's cart, proudly advertised his business philosophy. Leo never asked for charity, never took more than the stated price for his wares. Independent and free, he had achieved his goals. He never looked upon himself with pity and revulsion. Though imprisoned in his body, he found ways to transcend it. Actions most would call normal— driving, speaking, typing, reading—were, to Leo, marvelous goals attained only by supreme effort.

But Leo attained. He drove his tractor 30,000 miles until his vision failed at age sixty-two. For several more years, blind and deaf in a rest home, he hand-made leather purses to sell.

As a legacy, Leo left his thoughts, painstakingly typed:

"I think everyone at times feels lonesome, sorry for himself. But I'm not a quitter. Once weak and sickly, I'm now doing what no one thought possible. I'm in business for myself, enjoying life.

"Do I believe in the goodness of God? You all know the Bible saying, "We know to them that love God all things work together for good." So from my experiences in the past and to this very day, I can answer you truthfully, I most certainly do."

None of us could have quoted that verse to Leo Beuerman and comforted him in the midst of his adversity, because few have felt his kind of suffering. But the fact that Leo could still affirm God's goodness is a tribute to the truth that God's strength is made perfect in weakness.

When Jesus' disciples asked about a blind man, Jesus first denied that the blindness was punishment for any sin. Then He said, "This happened so that the work of God might be displayed in his life" (John 9:3 NIV). In people like Mr. Buckley and Leo Beuerman, God's work is assuredly being displayed. We who stand on the outside watching the suffering of people of the world expect to find anger and bitterness. We wait for them to turn to God and lash out against Him for the inequities of life. Amazingly, they often find a solace in Him that puts us to shame.

_____ **The Great Reversal** _____

What in the condition of suffering causes this reversal, where pain can build up instead of destroy?

Jesus plainly taught that, in a sense, the world as seen from God's viewpoint is tilted in favor of the poor and the suffering. Sometimes called the "theology of reversal,"[2] this teaching can be seen in the Sermon on the Mount and in Jesus' statements that the first shall be last (Matt. 19:30; Mark 10:31; Luke 13:30); he who humbles himself will be exalted (Luke 14:11; 18:14) etc. "Let the greatest among you become as the youngest, and the leader as one who serves," Jesus commanded (Luke 22:26 RSV). The parables of the good Samaritan and the rich man and Lazarus aver the truth of this reversal of the world's order.

Could Jesus be repeating the biblical idea that man's self-sufficiency must be shattered—the same self-sufficiency which first reared its head in the Garden of Eden? Jesus reserved His strongest language to denounce the sins of pride and piousness. If self-sufficiency is the most fatal sin because it pulls us, as if by a magnet, from God, then indeed the suffering and the poor do have an advantage. Their dependence and lack of self-sufficiency are obvious to them every day. They must turn somewhere for strength, and sometimes that renewal is found in God. The enticing encumbrances of life—lust, pride, success, glamour—are too far from some to be striven for, and a tremendous roadblock to the kingdom is thus bulldozed. Leo Beuerman and Mr. Buckley had no great visions of wealth or popularity or free-wheeling romance. Those goals seemed beyond their reach, even if they had wanted them.

George MacDonald refers to this principle in his exposition on the Sermon on the Mount, especially the phrase "poor in spirit." He says,

> *The poor, the beggars in spirit, the humble men of heart, the unambitious, the unselfish; those who never despise men, and never seek their praises; the lowly, who see nothing to admire in themselves, therefore cannot seek to be admired of others; the men who give themselves away—these are the freemen of the kingdom, these are the citizens of the new Jerusalem.*
>
> *The men who are aware of their own essential poverty; not the men who are poor in friends, poor in influence, poor in acquirements, poor in money, but those who are poor in spirit,*

*who feel themselves poor creatures; who know
nothing to be pleased with themselves for, and
desire nothing to make them think well of themselves; who know that they need much to make
their life worth living, to make their existence
a good thing, to make them fit to live; these
humble ones are poor whom the Lord calls
blessed.*

*When a man says, I am low and worthless,
then the gate of the kingdom begins to open to
him, for there enter the true, and this man has
begun to know the truth concerning himself.
Whatever such a man has attained to, he
straightway forgets; it is part of him and behind
him. His business is with what he has not, with
the things that lie above and before him.*[3]

In this way, the poor clearly are blessed: their daily
lives more closely illustrate the humility required to
enter the kingdom. The Sermon on the Mount decla-
rations ("Blessed are the poor ... those who mourn ...
the weak ... the persecuted") are not sops thrown out
by Jesus to improve the self-images of the lower classes.
They are true statements which reflect the reality of the
kingdom.

The single saying of Jesus which the Bible records
more often than any other (four times) expresses a
paradoxical truth: "Whoever finds his life will lose it,
and whoever loses his life for my sake will find it."
Sometimes seeming tragedies, like pain and suffering,
can nudge us along the path to "losing our lives," and
we can thereby draw closer to God.

Again, John Donne captured the truth in a prayer from

his devotions.* It is a prayer which cannot be forced on those who suffer, and yet it is one which flowed from the pen of a dying man.

> O most gracious God, who perfects Your own purposes, You have reminded me by the first pain of this sickness that I must die. As it continued besieging my body, You further reminded me that I may die even now. With the first symptoms You awakened me. With further suffering You cast me down to call me up to Yourself. You clothed me with Yourself by stripping me of myself. By dulling my bodily senses to the red meats and pleasures of this world, You have sharpened my spiritual senses to the apprehension of Yourself.
>
> As my body dissolves, Lord, my soul is exalted toward You. Speed up the pace of that process. My taste has not gone away, but gone up to sit at David's table, to taste, and see, that the Lord is good. My stomach has gone up towards the supper of the Lamb with the saints in heaven. My knees are weak, but weak so that I can easily kneel and fix myself upon You. . . .
>
> And, O God, who appeared as a light in a bush, in the midst of these brambles and thorns of a sharp sickness, appear unto me so that I may see You and know You to be my God, ap-

*Author's paraphrase from John Donne's *Devotions*.

plying Yourself to me, even in these sharp and thorny times. Do this, O Lord, for His sake, who was no less the King of heaven for Your suffering Him to be crowned with thorns in this world.[4]

PART
3

✳

How Can
We Cope
With Pain?

*As gas in the body will counterfeit any disease, and seem
the stone, and seem the gout, so fear will counterfeit any
disease of the mind.*

John Donne
Devotions

* 11 *

Two Enemies
of Recovery

I have met people with
rheumatoid arthritis who
find it difficult to talk
about anything else. I have met others who will only
admit the pain after prodding and questioning. What
makes the difference?

Few of us will experience the sudden life-stopping
crush of pain which Brian Sternberg and Joni Eareckson
have sustained. And most of us will be spared the psychological pain endured by Mr. Buckley or Leo Beuerman. Our pains will come for briefer periods, with less
intensity. People, however, respond differently to pain.
Is there a way to predict a person's response to pain?

Can we learn how to prepare for pain, to lessen its impact? From these experiences of people who suffer intensely we can draw principles which could help each of us in coping with pain.

—————————— Degrees of Hurt ——————————
Medical scientists are discovering that our *attitude* about a particular pain is one of the chief factors in intensifying its effects.

Some pain—such as athletics or torture from an enemy interrogator—people perceive as necessary and so are willing to accept. In fact, we often deliberately inflict pain on ourselves for cosmetic reasons. For centuries, Chinese women bound their feet in order to appear beautiful. Americans pluck eyebrows, sustain searing sunburn, and undergo plastic surgery to improve faces, breasts, and buttocks—all to fit cultural standards of beauty. We actually gain approval by having these pains. Some pains, such as a hard massage, or "rolfing," and a cold shower, are viewed as pleasurable, expressing a zest for life.

It makes a difference, too, how much sympathy we receive for a particular pain. Throbbing war wounds for a veteran or tension headaches for a super-achiever in the business world can be worn as badges of courage, bringing satisfaction. More invisible, neglected pains, such as hemorrhoids, are lonely, irritating struggles. They elicit embarrassment, not sympathy, and that intensifies the pain.[1]

A *Sports Illustrated* article in 1976 explored the contrasting responses of athletes to pain. In a sport such as football or hockey, all participants are subjected to the same crowding body-checks, elbow-crunches, and bruising falls. Injuries to vulnerable regions like the knee are so common that it is the norm in a locker room to see thick red scars crisscrossing players' knees. Yet they give remarkably varied responses.

Some athletes succeed despite excruciating pain. Earl Monroe of basketball's Knicks ignores arthritis. Muhammad Ali has fought most of his career with hands that throb constantly in the ring. Tennis star Tony Roche, who once scrambled to the No. 2 ranking in the world, fights pain which kept him off the court for half of this decade.

The *Sports Illustrated* article quoted Dr. Robert Kerlan, a renowned orthopedist in sports.

> *The pain threshold is high among superstars or high-level athletes. I think this is most true in the contact sports. I don't know if these athletes can accept more, but they definitely don't feel pain as much. Whether this is acceptance, or the way they're put together, we don't know. I think it has much to do with the way an athlete is put together. You have to have a high pain threshold to play football, hockey, definitely for boxing. In the more skilled sports the pain threshold might be a little lower, although basketball demands heavy contact, and there the level is high. When you try to compare thresholds of football and baseball players, it's not really fair. A football player can play with a broken hand. It's hard for a baseball player even to play with a blister on the end of his finger.* [2]

Sports journalist Mark Kram visited athletes with antithetical responses to pain. Atlanta Falcon's football player Taz Anderson, who dropped out of sports because of pain, is today confused and bitter. Yet Merlin Olsen, another player who has sustained multiple injuries, chooses to ignore pain:

> *Man is an adaptable creature. One finds out what you can or cannot do. It's like walking into a barnyard. The first thing you smell is manure. Stand there for about five minutes and you don't smell it anymore. The same thing is true of a knee. You hurt that knee. You're conscious of it. But then you start to play at a different level. You change your run a little bit. Or you drive off a different leg. Maybe you alter your stance.*
>
> *That year after surgery on my knee, I had to have the fluid drained weekly. Finally, the membrane got so thick they almost had to drive the needle in it with a hammer. I got to the point where I just said, "Damn it, get the needle in there, and get that stuff out."*[3]

Thus, even pain which is taken on voluntarily, as in sports, can be filtered through different prisms of human response. It depends on the mental attitude of the sufferer. Did he choose the pain? How strong is his desire to overcome it: for example, will he be rewarded for enduring the pain? Plus, there are some physiological differences that affect the thresholds of pain we can bear.

For most of us, there are two major attitudes which can drastically affect our ability to withstand pain. Our response hinges largely on the presence of these attitudes.

_____ **Fear Factor** _____

Dr. Paul Brand illustrates the varying effects of pain by relating his experience as a medical technician in London during World War II. There, injured men shipped over from the Continent told him phenomenal stories of courage. Some who had taken shrapnel or bits of grenade in their bodies disregarded the pain to rush out under heavy fire and rescue their buddies. The British soldiers' spirits were so high that few went down immediately with injuries. Often they continued fighting until it became physically impossible. Brand treated these men, some with amputated limbs, some with enormous ulcerations as a result of their wounds.

Strangely, these heroes lost all bravery when time for antibiotic shots rolled around. Penicillin, a new discovery then, was primitively manufactured in the huge vats of a London distiller. Impure and slightly noxious, the drug was too irritating for the veins to receive large doses, so small doses were injected every three hours. The injection stung like acid.

Brand recalls being on night duty when the nurse came in at two o'clock with the penicillin tray. Moments before she entered, the men would wake from sleeping. They would lie in bed, eyes wide open, some shuddering. As they heard her approach, some would emit rueful groans. Adult men—the some daring soldiers who had risked their lives on the battlefield—would sob uncontrollably as the nurse approached them with the needle.

None of these men would argue that the prick of a needle dripping penicillin, painful though it was, exceeded their suffering on the war front. But other factors—their surroundings and anticipations—made the experience of a single penicillin shot more horrifying than that life-and-death conflict.

Fear seems to be the single common denominator which can push a painful experience into the realm of the unbearable. Asenath Petrie, a researcher at the University of Chicago, has developed a fascinating system of classifying people into three categories by their response to pain (described in her book, *The Individuality of Pain and Suffering*). "Augmenters" have a low threshold of pain; any pain they experience is severely exaggerated. "Reducers" have a higher threshold of pain and can tolerate much more without noticeable disturbance. "Moderates" fall between. She found that fear is the single factor which best describes the augmenters' approach toward pain.

John Donne, after noting signs of fear in his attending physician, wrote down this description of the strength of fear.

> *Fear insinuates itself in every action or passion of the mind, and as gas in the body will counterfeit any disease, and seem the stone, and seem the gout, so fear will counterfeit any disease of the mind. It shall seem love, a love of having; and it is but a fear, a jealous and suspicious fear of losing. It shall seem valour, in despising and undervaluing danger, and it is but fear in an overvaluing of opinion and estimation and a fear of losing that. A man that is not afraid of a lion is afraid of a cat; not afraid of starving, and yet is afraid of some joint*

*of meat at the table presented to feed him. . . . I
know not what fear is, nor I know not what it
is that I fear now; I fear not the hastening of my
death, and yet I do fear the increase of the disease; I should belie nature if I should deny that
I feared this.* [4]

_____ Helplessness _____

In 1957, Dr. Curt Richter, a psychologist from Johns
Hopkins University, used two wild rats in a rather per-
verse experiment. He dropped Rat One into a tank of
warm water. Since rats are good swimmers, the creature
struggled and paddled for sixty hours before finally suc-
cumbing to exhaustion, when it promptly drowned.
Richter treated Rat Two differently. Before dropping it
in the water, he held it tightly in his hand until it stopped
struggling. When he dropped it in the tank, it reacted
remarkably differently. After splashing around for a few
minutes, it passively sank to the bottom of the tank.
Richter claims that Rat Two "gave up," convinced its
fate was hopeless even before he released it in the
water. [5] In effect, it died of resigned helplessness, the
second feeling which can characterize people who suffer and which can lead people to despair.

Strong feelings of fear or helplessness not only
worsen a sick patient's condition, they actually may
make healthy people more susceptible to illness. Dr.
Robert Ader, a professor of psychiatry and psychology
at Rochester School of Medicine, is one scientist who
believes practically all illnesses have emotional factors.
He concludes, "The germ theory simply can't account
for why people get sick, because if it could—I don't

know how big your office is, but if somebody gets the flu then I don't understand why everybody doesn't get it."[6]

Dozens of comprehensive studies have established this fact. One famous study, called "Broken Heart," researched the mortality rate of 4,500 widowers within six months of their wives' deaths. Compared with other men the same age, the widowers had a mortality rate 40 percent higher.[7]

In an article summarizing the effects of helplessness, *New York* magazine cites the example given by Major F. J. Harold Kushner, an army medical officer held by the Viet Cong for five-and-a-half years.

> *Among the prisoners in Kushner's POW camp was a tough young marine, 24 years old, who had already survived two years of prison-camp life in relatively good health. Part of the reason for this was that the camp commander had promised to release the man if he cooperated. Since this had been done before with others, the marine turned into a model POW and the leader of the camp's thought-reform group. As time passed he gradually realized that his captors had lied to him. When the full realization of this took hold he became a zombie. He refused to do all work, rejected all offers of food and encouragement, and simply lay on his cot sucking his thumb. In a matter of weeks he was dead.*[8]

Dr. Martin Seligman of the University of Pennsylvania attributes the young marine's death to helplessness. He feels that a strictly medical explanation of his decline into death isn't adequate. "Hope of release sustained him," Seligman writes. "When he gave up hope, when he believed that all his efforts had failed and would continue to fail, he died."[9]

The young marine's experience is a tragic, negative example of the need for some hope to live for. He contrasts with Brian Sternberg and Joni Eareckson as well as the concentration camp survivors introduced in the next chapter. But he represents thousands of people—including many people who are old, divorced, lonely, or poor—who succumb to a feeling of helplessness.

Pain itself—not just the psychological attitude, but the physical experience of hurt—can be likewise affected by a patient's attitude toward it, or by his feeling of helplessness. In some experiments measuring pain thresholds, scientists found that the pain threshold went up from 19 to 45 percent just by diverting the attention of the research subject. In other words, in a test where heat was focused on a subject's arm, it took 19 to 45 percent more applied heat before the preoccupied subject noted pain. Researchers diverted attention by clanging bells, repeatedly touching the subject's hand, reading an adventure story aloud, and having the subject read numbers. If he had nothing to do all day but think about his pain (as is true in many hospitals and nursing homes), the pain was much more oppressive.[10]

A warning, then, to any person facing prolonged illness, is to look for ways to avoid feelings of helplessness. It is essential for handicapped people, for example, to be given tools so they can restore activity. British engineers have invented a device called Possum by which a totally paralyzed person can operate a wheelchair, type, and turn on a TV or stereo, all by using his breath. By various combinations of sucking and blowing, he signals the machine. Such devices can spell the difference between recovery and despair. Brian Sternberg's amateur radio hobby and Joni Eareckson's artwork are probably more crucial to their attitudes than even the support of caring friends.

The next chapter will introduce ways we can combat helplessness and fear in ourselves and in suffering people around us. These rules, drawn from the common experiences of survivors, can help prevent the failure of spirit which destroyed the young marine.

In my sleep pain falls drop by drop upon my heart until in my agony—the grace of God is revealed.

Aeschylus

** 12 **

Preparations

On Good Friday, 1964, a violent earthquake rocked Alaska, smashing homes, obliterating streets, and unleashing tidal waves. Families were separated, 117 people died, and $750 million in property was destroyed.

Sociologists swooped down on cities like Anchorage and Seward, near the quake's epicenter, to analyze human reactions. After interviewing hundreds of survivors and tracking them over the next few years, the research teams came up with these conclusions:

1) On the whole, Alaskans responded beautifully to the crisis. There was little panic and no looting, and

survivors showed compassion to each other. The communities rebounded quickly from the effects of the disaster. The sociologists concluded Alaskans did well because they were used to handling adversity; they needed a pioneer spirit just to survive the harsh conditions of their state.

2) Those who stayed through the six months of aftershocks adapted best to the crisis. Traumatized families who fled the state immediately after the initial quake had higher rates of divorce and emotional instability. It seemed to help overcome fear to stay and face reminders of the disaster.

3) Family members who were together at the moment of the quake fared better than families who were scattered in different locations—schools, shopping centers, etc.

4) A majority of people turned to God with a dramatic prayer. Church attendance swelled to record numbers, but within a year it had dropped back to normal.

Scientists expertly analyze how people respond to disasters, after the fact, yet little of the information is compacted into usable, life-changing form to help us prepare for our own crises.

Each crisis points up the main enemies of fear and helplessness (or despair)—factors which Alaskans evidently had some experience in coping with.

_____ Survivors _____

What resources can we offer suffering people in our lives to combat feelings of helplessness and fear? Current medical science allows more reason for hope than ever before in history. Yet medicine can do little to change the attitudes of patients. If fear and helplessness are such critical factors in one's response, we should explore specific ways to counteract those feelings.

A suffering person desperately needs some resources which any of us can give: love, hope, a sense of presence. Our efforts to help, then, should be directed toward giving the person's spirit the strength it needs to counteract the devastating attack on his body. Those men who survive pain with their spirits stronger—men such as Stanley Stein, who described his fight against Hansen's disease in *No Longer Alone*, and Alexander Solzhenitsyn, whose concentration camp experiences are told in *The Gulag Archipelago*—are stirring tributes to the resilience of the human spirit. In these rare persons, suffering actually fed the spirit, nourishing it and toughening it.

Once again we must turn to extreme situations to distill principles of coping which can apply to our own lesser hurts. How can we counteract the sense of dread that permeates us with helplessness? Concentration camp experiences, especially, reveal that helplessness can be overcome under the least humane circumstances.

Terence Des Pres, in *The Survivors*, reviewed most of the literature written by survivors of the Holocaust. As he studied actual records of those who lived, he found the myth that Jews were "led like sheep to the slaughter," meekly accepting their fates, was largely unfounded. Behind the barbed wire and brick walls, the besieged Jews developed a new range of expressing human courage and kindness. Some, of course, succumbed. But others resisted and refused to let the Nazis crush their human spirits. If you attend a meeting of the survivors of the Holocaust today, you will not find defeated, useless human beings who walk about like zombies. You will find politicians, doctors, lawyers.

Des Pres refers to the Nazi attempt to create the ultimate "Skinner box" of behaviorism, where environment was engineered to reduce inmates to mindless creatures whose behavior could be predicted and controlled. The camps used pain and death as "negative reinforcers" and food and life as "positive reinforcers," applying them consistently and horribly. Yet, the experiment did not succeed. Some prisoners gave in, some withdrew, but many resisted and found their own ways of coping.

Some survivors of such camps emerged, not with the warped, distorted view of cruelty and inhumanity you might expect, but with a resurrected concept of virtue and hope (examples: Corrie ten Boom and those described in Solzhenitsyn's accounts). One such man is George Mangakis, who was inhumanly tortured and sentenced to eighteen years as a political prisoner during the recent military junta in Greece. Mangakis was helped by holding to his ethical beliefs and by pitying his torturer, not himself.

> I have experienced the fate of a victim. I have seen the torturer's face at close quarters. It was in a worse condition than my own bleeding, livid face. The torturer's face was distorted by a kind of twitching that had nothing human about it. . . .
>
> In this situation, I turned out to be the lucky one. I was humiliated. I did not humiliate others. I was simply bearing a profoundly unhappy hu-

*manity in my aching entrails. Whereas the men
who humiliate you must first humiliate the notion of humility within themselves. Never mind
if they strut around in their uniforms, swollen
with the knowledge that they can control the
suffering, sleeplessness, hunger and despair of
their fellow human beings, intoxicated with the
power in their hands. Their intoxication is nothing other than the degradation of humanity. The
ultimate degradation. They have had to pay
very dearly for my torments.*

*I wasn't the one in the worst position. I was
simply a man who moaned because he was in
great pain. I prefer that. At this moment I am
deprived of the joy of seeing children going to
school or playing in the parks. Whereas they
have to look their own children in the face.* [1]

_____ **A Thread of Help** _____

Mangakis survived by an idealism which allowed him
to rise above his captors. Because of his belief in humanity, he came to view his torturers with pity. Few,
however, can sustain that kind of inner reserve. More
commonly, family is the crucial focus of hope among
sufferers. In Nazi camps, those who knew of family members still free would cling to the hope of someday being
reunited.

In fact, the type of visceral hope required to survive
a concentration camp experience was often possible
only when the inmate knew someone *cared* ultimately
what happened to him. Nazi guards tried to break up
strong friendships by separating friends and encour-

aging inmates to turn each other in for violations.

There are parallels in the less extreme encounters with suffering in the "normal" world. Most people in great pain, physical or psychological, express a strong feeling of aloneness. They seem abandoned, by God and by others, because they must bear the pain themselves and no one else quite understands.

Reading accounts of the Holocaust has impressed upon me the enormous importance of reaching out to those in pain with a thread of empathy. Suffering people often erect barriers which complicate this process. "You'll never understand; you've never been through something like this," they say.

In those cases, a person who has been through a similar experience may offer help. Joni Eareckson was jarred from self-pity when she received a hospital visit from a cheerful, radiant quadriplegic (and now she continues the chain by bringing hope to others). Father Damien found that his ministry among those with leprosy in Molokai, Hawaii, only became effective after he had contracted the disease and could relate as a fellow-sufferer. Hospitals have wisely begun instituting programs whereby a woman facing a mastectomy or a man facing surgery for cancer can be visited by patients who have lived through those experiences.

Sufferings can become a trap for self-pity, wounded pride, martyr feelings, and a negative self-image. Other people can represent the only way to help a person climb out of his helpless despair.

I have filled the middle part of this book with illustrations of people who have "successfully coped" with suffering. There are, of course, many examples of people destroyed by pain. But hope is such a crucial ingredient in coping with pain that I wonder if realistic "success stories" can be overemphasized. We healthy people tire of the typical "handicapped person finds happiness and usefulness" stories in *Reader's Digest* and *Saturday Evening Post*. But the handicapped people I've talked with view those stories much more solemnly. The survivors challenge their condition.

_____ **Grief Embraced** _____

I would gladly pay thousands of dollars for physical therapy if my wife was permanently disabled. I would do the same for a close friend in need. But will I invest the time necessary to give myself to spiritual or emotional therapy? Suffering people often need a step-by-step repatterning of the psyche: a new belief in themselves, a new identity, a new niche in the world where they're confidently appreciated.

A pastor in the Midwest wrote me about an experience he had several years ago, a "nervous breakdown" the doctors called it.

> *The most painful part of it was the seeming silence of God. I prayed, I thought, to a silent darkness. I have thought a lot about this. He only seemed silent. The problem was partly my depression and partly the Christian community. For most Christians I was an embarrassment. Nothing they said dealt with what I endured. One pastor prayed for me in generalities and pieties that were utterly unrelated to the situation. They would not feel my pain.*
>
> *Other people just avoided me. Ironically, Job's friends were probably a help to him, psy-*

chologically. At least they forced out feelings,
even if angry ones. Their pronouncements were
useless, but they did deal with the questions and
gave Job the impression that maybe God was
around somewhere. No one in the Christian
community, except my wife, helped me even to
that degree.

Years later the same pastor, with renewed mental
health, was reading Psalm 145 from the pulpit. He tried
to concentrate, but something was plaguing him: his
week-old grandson had just died, grieving the whole
family. He couldn't continue reading the words about
God's goodness and fairness. His voice choked, he
stopped reading, and he told the tense congregation
what had happened.

"As people left the church," he remembers, "they said
two important and helpful things:

1. 'Thank you for sharing your pain with us.'

2 'I grieve with you.' This simple statement was the
most helpful thing said. I did not feel alone. Unlike during the time of depression before, I was not abandoned
by God and His people. They embraced my grief."

Sometimes a simple expression, a web of shared pain,
is all we can offer—not a smile and a "Praise the Lord!"

_____ Hope for Healing _____

There's one important aspect of the problem of pain
which I have avoided. I haven't emphasized miraculous
healing in this book for two reasons. First, there are
many good books on healing available, ranging from
personal testimonies to theological treatises. Second,
I'm writing about people trapped in pain who are ques-

tioning God. Healing is one way out of the dilemma, but it's not for everyone. Ask Brian Sternberg.

I don't mean to downplay physical healing. I'm sure if a doctor diagnosed cancer in me tomorrow, I would plunge down every avenue toward healing. But everyone who has been healed (and also those who have been used to heal others) eventually dies. So healing does not remove the problem of pain; it merely delays it.

A hope for healing can start as a great antidote for helplessness, for it gives the sufferer a potential goal. In the unusual case of Brian Sternberg, it has kept his faith alive for a decade and a half.

Yet a hope for healing, if it is not rewarded and God chooses not to heal, can be a great impediment to faith. It can worsen the helpless despair. Let me give an example. Barbara Sanderville, a young paraplegic writer in Minnesota, described this process in a letter to me:

> Someone told me just after I became a Christian that God would heal me. This seemed too good to be true, and I didn't know if I dared believe it. But seeing nothing in the Bible that contradicted it, I began to hope, and then to believe. But my faith was shaky, and when Christians came along and said, "God doesn't heal everyone," or "Affliction is a cross we must bear," my faith would waver. Then last fall it just seemed to die. I gave up believing God would heal me.
>
> At that point in my life I knew I couldn't face spending the rest of my life in the wheelchair. Knowing that God had the power to heal me but wouldn't (or so I thought) made me very

bitter. I would read Isaiah 53, and 1 Peter 2:24, and accuse God of holding the promise of healing before me like a piece of meat before a starving dog. He tempted me by showing the potential but never quite allowing me to reach it. This in turn produced deep guilt feelings because from the Bible I knew God was a loving God and answerable to no man. I had such a conflict in me that my mental state was precarious and I thought of suicide many times.

I began to take tranquilizers just to get through the day as my guilt and resentment built a higher and higher wall between God and me. About this time I began having headaches and problems with my eyes. An opthalmologist could find no physical reason.

I was still praying because I knew God was alive, but I usually ended up crying and railing out at God. I'm afraid I experienced a lot of self-pity, which was very destructive. And over and over I asked God why He wouldn't heal me when it so plainly says that healing is a part of the redemption plan.

Barbara eventually found a mental healing that swept away the bitterness. She is still awaiting physical healing.

Because of experiences like Barbara's, I believe a hope for healing should be presented realistically. It is just that—a "hope," not a guarantee. If it comes, a joyous miracle has happened. If it doesn't come—God has not let you down. He can use even the infirmity to produce good within you.

_____ **Losing Fear** _____

To many areas of the problem of pain, Christianity offers what seem to be incomplete answers. Sometimes, as with Barbara, Christian principles seem confusing and paradoxical. A personal faith can, however, better equip a person to cope with fear, the second key factor in any response to pain.

By their nature experiences of overcoming fear are individual, not uniform. I could say, "Banish fear by trusting God," but what help is that? How does one go about it?

The Bible is a Christian's guidebook, and I believe the knowledge it sheds on pain and suffering is the great antidote to fear for suffering people. Knowledge can dissolve fear as light destroys darkness.

When I suffer pain over any length of time I try to reflect on the good which the Bible has promised pain is producing in me. In one such list, Romans 5:1–5, Paul lists perseverance, character, hope, and confidence or boldness.

"How does suffering accomplish these?" I ask myself. It produces perseverance, or steadiness, by slowing me down, by forcing me to turn to God, by proving to me that I can survive a crisis. As for character—the last few chapters were full of examples of how people grew in character through suffering. I continue through the list, asking how God can be involved in the suffering process.

The confidence that God can use suffering to produce these qualities is very comforting. Knowing that suffering is temporary and will someday be rewarded—that's the topic of chapter 15, but it can also be a key to stabilizing faith under trial.

The Bible is filled with resources available to one trying to stave off fears and helplessness. Reading Job's thrashings in fear about God's seeming lack of concern can make mine easier to bear. The history of God's love and goodness throughout the Bible can salve my doubts. And knowledge about prayer to a loving God can ward off frenzied efforts to "muster up faith" in hopes of impressing God—prayer does not work that way, as the Bible shows. God is already full of loving concern; we do not need to impress Him with spiritual calisthenics.

Knowledge about pain itself, its medical functions, also can help to diminish fear. To me, the most encouraging factor in coping with suffering has been the knowledge I've gained in seeing pain's contributions, mainly through Dr. Brand's research. This book flows out of my own discovery. Suffering is much less fearful now that I understand its role and value.

_____ Serving Others _____

Psychologist Thomas Malone of the Atlantic Psychiatric Clinic says he meets two kinds of people. One group is unhealthy and studded with inadequacies. These people walk around crying, "Please love me, please love me." The other group is composed of people whole enough to be lovers. He says that the best cure for the first group is to help them to the point where *they* can be lovers and helpers of others. If they reach the place of being helpers, they will automatically fill the deep needs for attention and love inside them.

I think there is a parallel situation among suffering people. Psychiatrists and counselors have found if they can get patients to see themselves as helpers and givers, instead of always receivers, healing may follow.

Joni Eareckson described to me her shock in discovering that many of the handicapped people in her rehabilitation home stayed there voluntarily. It seemed easier to remain among people who accepted their condition than to risk the "outside" world. She became a leader to them, working at her exercises, inspiring hope, and *wanting* to be released. The very process of pouring herself into their needs proved therapeutic. She herself became stronger. Her self-concept improved, and she stopped thinking of herself as a pitiable sufferer.

Brian Sternberg went through a similar emotional process as he began speaking at FCA conferences across the country, and Leo Beuerman found his fulfillment in his business.

_____ **Waiting for Pain** _____

This book opened with the experience of Claudia Claxton, who suddenly found herself battling Hodgkin's disease and the specter of death. I talked at length with Claudia and her husband John on why their crisis actually pulled them together, whereas some crises push marriage partners farther apart.

What kept fear and helplessness from splitting their close relationship? John had the additional insight of working as a chaplain's assistant in a hospital where he observed people responding to suffering and death. "I have seen dying patients in hospitals," John told me. "It's not like on the TV shows and in the movies like *Airport*. In the movies, couples who have fought for years, in the face of danger, suddenly forget their differences and come together. Life doesn't work that way, however.

"When a couple meets a crisis, the result is a caricature of what's already there in their relationship. We happened to deeply love each other and had open communication. Therefore the crisis drove us to each other. We were unified and we trusted each other. Feelings of blame and anger against each other did not creep in. The crisis of Claudia's illness merely brought to the surface and magnified feelings already present."

According to John, the best way to prepare for a crisis is to have a strong, supportive life when you're healthy. Mental suffering and physical pain merely warn us of a problem; they are characteristics of disease, not the disease itself. You cannot suddenly fabricate foundations of strength from nowhere; they must have been building all along. If you learn a pattern of depending on others and sharing yourself when healthy, it will be a more natural response when you're in pain.

A common illustration of that process is seen in the diverse ways people prepare for old age, a period of great psychological suffering. There is a saying, "The young get the face they are born with; the old get the face they deserve." The life we have lived crystallizes into the less flexible personality of old age. During old age, the body deteriorates. We realize we are no longer able to do the things we once could. We shrink from mirrors, because beauty has been replaced by thinning hair, wrinkles, and skin discoloration. Friends die, we become a burden to the family, and it's easy to view the time as a waiting for death, a time when nothing is contributed to life, only taken away.

J. Robertson McQuilkin, president of Columbia Bible College, was once approached by an elderly lady facing these trials. "Robertson, why does God let us get old and weak? Why must I hurt so?" she asked him.

After a few moments' thought he replied, "I think God has planned the strength and beauty of youth to be physical. But the strength and beauty of age is spiritual. We gradually lose the strength and beauty that is temporary so we'll be sure to concentrate on the strength and beauty which is forever. And so we'll be eager to leave the temporary, deteriorating part of us and be truly homesick for our eternal home. If we stayed young and strong and beautiful, we might never want to leave!"

If there is a secret to handling suffering, the one most often cited by those I interviewed was along this line. To survive, the spirit must be fed so that it is freed beyond the body and will ultimately triumph. Christian faith does not always offer resources to the body. Neither Brian Sternberg nor Joni Eareckson has been healed, despite thousands of prayers. Yet God does promise supernatural strength to the spirit. When we have nothing else to lean on, not even ourselves, He is still there.

In speaking to His followers, Jesus constantly stressed to them a new view of life, one that emphasized the spirit and not the body. "Do not be afraid of those who can only kill your body; they cannot kill your soul," He said as He sent them out. Paul, taking up this theme, wrote, "I am caught from both sides: I want very much to leave this life and be with Christ, which is a far better thing; but it is much more important, for your sake, that I remain alive" (Phil. 1:23, 24 TEV).

Fox's Book of Martyrs is generally viewed as a quaint, trumped-up tale of people who sought attention through suffering. Anyone who reads it carefully, however, must be impressed by the truth in the phrase "the blood of martyrs was the seed of the church." In Christianity a new thought entered the world: our bodies are habitations for an eternal spirit, and thus all suffering must be seen as temporary misfortune which damages only part of us. Fox records accounts of gruesome, unbelievable torture which saints endured with hymns of praise on their lips. They memorialize the triumph of spirit over body.

Pain is not merely a physical phenomenon. Attitudes of fear and helplessness affect the quantity of suffering. At least we have the inspiring examples of those who have proved that human spirit can ascend through the worst of circumstances. And because man is both body and spirit, Christianity can offer a true and healing hope.

I have never thought that a Christian would be free of suffering. For our Lord suffered. And I have come to believe that He suffered, not to save us from suffering, but to teach us how to bear suffering. For He knew that there is no life without suffering.

Alan Paton
Cry, the Beloved Country

* 13 *
The Preceder

Christianity offers one puzzling, almost paradoxical, contribution to those struggling with the problem of suffering. Some have obviously missed its message.

Hear an eloquent expression from the mouth of a migrant farmhand mother (as recorded by Robert Coles in his book, *Migrants, Sharecroppers and Mountaineers*).

Last year we went to a little church in New Jersey. . . . We had all our children there, the baby included. The Reverend Jackson was there, I can't forget his name, and he told us to be quiet, and he told us how glad we should be that we're in this country, because it's Christian, and not "godless." Then my husband went and lost his temper; something happened to his nerves, I do believe. He got up and started shouting, yes sir. He went up to the Reverend Mr. Jackson and told him to shut up and never speak again—not to us, the migrant people. He told him to go on back to his church, wherever it is, and leave us alone and don't be standing up there looking like he was so nice to be doing us a favor.

Then he did the worst thing he could do: he took the baby, Annie, and he held her right before his face, the minister's, and he screamed and shouted and hollered at him, that minister, like I've never before seen anyone do. I don't remember what he said, the exact words, but he told him that here was our little Annie, and she's never been to the doctor, and the child is sick . . . and we've got no money, not for Annie or the other ones or ourselves.

Then he lifted Annie up, so she was higher than the reverend, and he said why doesn't he go and pray for Annie and pray that the growers will be punished for what they're doing to us, all the migrant people. . . . And then my husband began shouting about God and His neglecting us while He took such good care of the other people all over.

Then the reverend did answer—and that was his mistake, yes it was. He said we should be careful and not start blaming God and criticizing Him and complaining to Him and like that, because God wasn't supposed to be taking care of the way the growers behave and how we live, here on this earth. "God worries about your future"; that's what he said, and I tell you, my husband

near exploded. He shouted about 10 times to the rev-
erend, "Future, future, future." Then he took Annie and
near pushed her in the reverend's face and Annie, she
started crying, poor child, and he asked the reverend
about Annie's "future" and asked him what he'd do if
he had to live like us, and if he had a "future" like ours.
Then he told the reverend he was like all the rest, making
money off us, and he held our Annie as high as he could,
right near the cross, and told God He'd better stop having
the ministers speaking for Him, and He should come and
see us for Himself, and not have the "preachers"—he
kept calling them the "preachers"—speaking for Him.

He stopped after he'd finished talking about the
"preachers" and he came back to us, and there wasn't
a sound in the church, no sir, not one you could hear—
until a couple of other men said he was right, my hus-
band was . . . and everyone clapped their hands and I
felt real funny. [1]

This migrant family sums up the dilemma of pain and
suffering about as well as it can be expressed. Why does
God allow a world of sick children and no money and
no hope? Their problem is not abstract and philosophical. It's human: their child Annie hurts, and they see
no solution. Does God care?

I wish I could give this farmhand family an answer to
their dilemma, but I can't. They need a solution to their
condition, not a mental answer. That won't come unless
someone responds to their needs with true love.

But I can say that on one point the angry farmhand
was dead wrong. Holding his child in front of the reverend's face, up near the cross, he demanded that God
come down and see for Himself what this world is like.

It's not enough, he said, for God to keep having the preachers speak for Him.

But, wait. God did come. He entered humanity, and believe me, He saw and felt for Himself what this world is like. Jesus took on the same kind of body you and I have. His nerve fibers were not bionic—they screamed pain when they were misused. And, above all men in history, Jesus was surely misused. This fact of history can have a large effect on the fear and helpless despair of sufferers. It helps us to cope with pain.

The Man Who Would Be King

Clear your mind and reflect, for a moment, on what you know of Jesus' life. The Bible says there is no temptation known to man which Jesus did not experience. He was lonely, tired, hungry, personally assaulted by Satan, besieged by leeching admirers, persecuted by powerful enemies.

Jesus was the only person in history who could plan His own birth. He humbled Himself, trading in a perfect heavenly body for a frail body of blood and sinew and cartilage.

When He was first beginning His ministry, the people hooted, "Can anything good come from Nazareth?" ... an ancient ethnic joke. Jesus, the hick, the country bumpkin from Nazareth.

And what did Jesus look like? There's only one physical description of Him in the entire Bible, written by the prophet Isaiah: "He had no beauty, no majesty to draw our eyes, no grace to make us delight in him" (Isa. 53:2 NEB).

His boyhood neighbors ran Him out of town and tried to kill Him. His friends questioned His sanity. The leaders of the day proudly reported that not one authority or religious leader believed Him. Those who followed Him were a motley crew of fishermen and peasants, among whom the migrant farmhand would have felt comfortably at home.

The promises Jesus made must have seemed especially empty to the people who lived in His day. At the end, He was standing before Pilate, a perplexed Roman governor. Outside, the masses were yelling, "Kill him! Kill him!" He who had healed so many others would not save Himself.

This man a king? A mock king if ever there was one. Someone had thrown a fine, purple robe over Him, but blood from Pilate's beatings streaked down His back and legs, clotting on the cloth.

More unlikely—this man God? Even to His disciples, who had loved Him and followed Him for three years, the prospects were dim. They hung back in the crowd, afraid to be identified with the mock king. Their dreams of a powerful ruler who could banish pain and suffering in the world turned into nightmares.

The scene, with the sharp spikes and bleeding death and wrenching thud as the cross was dropped in the ground, has been told so often, that we, who shrink from a news story on the death of a race horse or of baby seals, flinch not at all at its retelling. It was a bloody death, an execution quite unlike the quick, sterile ones we know today—gas chambers, electric chairs, hangings. This one stretched on for hours in front of a jeering crowd.

Jesus' humanity and the weight that He bore crashed to the surface when at the peak of His agony He, the teacher of prayer, suddenly realized His own prayers were going unheard. Deserted by men, He found Himself deserted by God and cried out, "My God, my God, why have You forsaken me?" It was as if the earth convulsed. The ground shook, rocks shattered, graves spilled out bodies long dead, and the sun was hidden from earth for three hours. Incredibly, the Creator of the universe demonstrated one last human quality, the quality of courage, which no omnipotent Sovereign would normally be called on to experience. His soul passed a breaking point, but it did not break.

Jesus' death is the cornerstone of the Christian faith, the most important fact of His coming. You can't follow Jesus without confronting His death: the Gospels bulge with its details. He laid out a trail of hints and bald predictions about it throughout His ministry, predictions that were only understood after the thing had been done, when to the disciples the dream looked shattered. His life seemed prematurely wasted. His triumphant words from the night before surely must have cruelly haunted His followers as they watched Him groan and twitch on the cross.

_____ No Longer Alone _____
What possible contribution to the problem of pain and suffering could come from a religion based on an event like the Crucifixion? There, God Himself succumbed to pain.

I can think of one contribution. We are not abandoned. The farmhand with the sick child, the swollen six-year-old with leukemia, the grieving relatives in Yuba City, the leprosy patients in Louisiana—none has to suffer alone. Because God came, He fully understands.

The image Jesus left with the world, the cross, the most common image in the Christian region, is proof that God cares about our suffering and pain. He died of it. Today the image is coated with gold and worn around the necks of beautiful girls, a symbol of how far we can stray from the reality of history. But it stands, unique among all the religions of the world. Many of them have gods. But only one has a God who cared enough to become a man and to die.

Dorothy Sayers says:

> *For whatever reason God chose to make man as he is—limited and suffering and subject to sorrows and death—He had the honesty and courage to take His own medicine. Whatever game He is playing with His creation, He has kept His own rules and played fair. He can exact nothing from man that He has not exacted from Himself. He has Himself gone through the whole of human experience, from the trivial irritations of family life and the cramping restrictions of hard work and lack of money to the worst horrors of pain and humiliation, defeat, despair, and death. When He was a man, He played the man. He was born in poverty and died in disgrace and thought it well worthwhile.* [2]

To some, the image of a pale body glimmering on a dark night whispers of defeat. What good is a God who does not control His Son's suffering? What possible good could such a God do for us? But a louder sound can be heard: the shout of a God crying out to man "I LOVE YOU." Love was compressed for all history in that lonely, bleeding figure. Jesus, who had said He could call down angels at any moment and rescue Himself from the horror, chose not to—because of us. For God so loved us, that He sent His only Son to die for us.

And thus the cross, an eternal stumbling block to some, became the cornerstone of our faith. Any discussion of how pain and suffering fit into God's system ultimately leads back to the cross.

By taking it on Himself, Jesus in a sense dignified pain. Of all the kinds of lives He could have lived, He chose a suffering one. Because of Jesus, I can never say about a person, "He must be suffering because of some sin he committed"; Jesus, who did not sin, also felt pain. And I cannot say, "Suffering and death must mean God has forsaken us; He's left us alone to self-destruct." Because even though Jesus died, His death became the great victory of history, pulling man and God together. God made a supreme good out of that awful day.

Jesus' followers are not insulated from the tragedies of this world, just as He was not. God has never promised that tornados will skip our houses on the way to our pagan neighbors'. Microbes do not flee from Christians bodies. Rather, Peter could say to suffering Christians, "This suffering is all part of the work God has given you. Christ, who suffered for you, is your example. Follow in his steps" (1 Peter 2:21 LB). The Bible goes further, using phrases I will not attempt to explain such as "partakers in His suffering" and "complete His suffering," indicating that suffering can be, not a horror to be shed at all costs, but a means of grace to make us more like God.

_____ **Jesus' Reminders** _____

What practical effect does Christ's identification have on the person who actually suffers? We have already seen two examples in Brian Sternberg and Joni Eareckson. Both described scenes when they derived critical strength when they realized the God they serve also endured pain. A dramatic example of the effect of this truth was seen in the ministry of Dr. Paul Brand while he was working among leprosy patients in Vellore, India. There he preached a sermon,* one of his best known and best loved. At that time, Brand and his workers were among the few in the area who would touch or closely approach a person with Hansen's disease— townspeople quarantined them. Brand slipped in late to a patients' gathering, sitting on a mat at the edge of an open courtyard. The air was heavy with combined odors of crowding bodies, poverty, stale spices, treated bandages.

The patients insisted on a few words from Dr. Brand, and he reluctantly agreed. He stood for a moment, empty of ideas, looking at the patients before him. His eyes were drawn to their hands, dozens of them, most pulled inward in the familiar "leprosy claw-hand," some with no fingers, some with a few stumps. Many patients sat on their hands or otherwise hid them from view.

"I am a hand surgeon," he began, and waited for the translation into Tamil and Hindi. "So when I meet people, I can't help looking at their hands. The

*Following description partially derived from _Ten Fingers for God_ by Dorothy Clarke Wilson.

palmist claims he can tell your future by looking at your hands. I can tell your past. For instance, I can tell what your trade has been by the position of the calluses and the condition of the nails. I can tell a lot about your character; I love hands."

He paused and looked at the eager faces. "How I would love to have had the chance to meet Christ and study His hands! But knowing what He was like, I can almost picture them, feel them."

He paused again, then wondered aloud what it would have been like to meet Christ and study His hands. He traced the hands of Christ, beginning with infancy when His hands were small, helpless, futilely grasping. Then came the hands of the boy Jesus, clumsily holding a brush or stylus, trying to form letters of the alphabet. Then the hands of Christ the carpenter—rough, gnarled, with broken fingernails and bruises from working with a saw and hammer.

Then there were the hands of Christ the physician, the healer. Compassion and sensitivity seemed to radiate from them, so much so that when He touched people they could feel something of the divine spirit coming through. Christ touched the blind, the diseased, the needy.

"Then," continued Dr. Brand, "there were His crucified hands. It hurts me to think of a nail being driven through the center of my hand, because I know what goes on there, the tremendous complex of tendons and nerves and blood vessels and muscles. It's impossible to drive a spike through its center without crippling it. The thought of those healing hands being crippled reminds me of what Christ was prepared to endure. In that act He identified Himself with all the deformed and crippled human beings in the world. Not only was He able to endure poverty with the poor, weariness with the tired, but—clawed hands with the crippled."

The effect on the listening patients, all social outcasts, was electrifying. Jesus...a cripple, with a claw-hand like theirs?

Brand continued. "And then there were His resurrected hands. One of the things I find most astounding is that, though we think of the future life as something perfected, when Christ appeared to His disciples He said, 'Come look at my hands,' and he invited Thomas to put his finger into the print of the nail. Why did He want to keep the wounds of His humanity? Wasn't it because He wanted to carry back with Him an eternal reminder of the sufferings of those on earth? He carried the marks of suffering so He could continue to understand the needs of those suffering. He wanted to be forever one with us."

As he finished, Paul Brand was again conscious of hands as they were lifted, all over the courtyard, palm to palm in the Indian gesture of respect, *namaste*. The hands were the same stumps, the same missing fingers, and crooked arches. Yet no one tried to hide them. They were held high, close to the face, in respect for Brand, but also with new pride and dignity. God's own response to suffering made theirs easier.

T. S. Eliot wrote in one of his *Four Quartets*:

> *The wounded surgeon plies the steel*
> *That questions the distempered part;*
> *Beneath the bleeding hands we feel*

*The sharp compassion of the healer's art
Resolving the enigma of the fever chart.*[3]

The surgery of life hurts. It hurts me, though, to know that the Surgeon Himself, the Wounded Surgeon, has felt every stab of pain and every sorrow.

I do not ask the wounded person how he feels, I myself become the wounded person.

Walt Whitman

* 14 *

The Rest of the Body

Even with the example of His life, death, and resurrection, Jesus' mission on earth was not complete. "I will build My church," He had declared, "and the gates of hell will not prevail against it."

For almost 2000 years now, the church has been without Christ's visible presence. We cannot take people to a village in the Middle East to have our Leader heal them. Rather, He left His message with small cells of believers who gathered together to worship Him. Reflecting on the role of the church without its visible leader, Paul reached for the analogy of the body of

Christ—which, to me, is one of the most satisfying analogies in all of the Bible. Christ is the invisible head, Paul said, and we are all members of His body. We are organically linked with the rest of the church, and, like the billions of individual cells in our body, each of us can affect the health and survival of the entire body.

What are the implications of this analogy? Are there parallels to the pain network in the body of Christ?

The Servant King

All Christians are familiar with the notion of Christ as Lord. We understand how He, as head of the body, directs His church in the world. But have we neglected another facet to the analogy—the limits of being head?

It is an awesome and mysterious truth that in a strange way God has limited Himself. By choosing to be not the entire body but the invisible head, Jesus is in some ways servant of the body.

Even during His life on earth Jesus was preparing us. What role did He take delight in? Not the role of performer of supernatural acts—I have previously mentioned Jesus' tendency to "hush up" miracles, performing them sometimes reluctantly. But Luke 10 records a clear case of what excited Jesus. First, He sent seventy followers to the surrounding villages and waited. When they returned and reported outstanding victories, such as casting out demons, Jesus uttered a stream of exultation and spontaneous praise. He was genuinely thrilled.

Jesus Himself did not do the job of the seventy; He merely gave them instructions and sent them out. The experiment succeeded, proving His work could be carried on by His inexperienced followers.

Jesus' plan was to leave the message of the gospel in the hands of flawed, bumbling men. He limited Himself as the head of the church. He left the arms, legs, ears, eyes, and voice to a disheveled group of disciples ... and to you and me.

Jesus' decision to operate as head of a large body affects our view of suffering. It means that He often uses us to help one another cope with suffering. In one sense, pain is a private struggle which no one can help us bear. But a body offers a context within which individual pains can be cared for, treated, and perhaps healed.

Physical pain is effective because it forces the body to cease other activities and attend to the reason for the pain. If a basketball player breaks a wrist, he must leave the game and treat it until it heals. In the same way, we members of Christ's body should learn to attend to the pains of the rest of the body. We can become the emotional incarnation of Christ's risen body. Just as the world will never learn the Good News apart from our efforts, the church of Christ will never experience a healing response to suffering unless we learn to focus on the body's pains and act as healing agents.

Dr. Paul Brand has developed this idea as a key part of his personal philosophy.

> *Individual cells had to give up their autonomy and learn to suffer with one another before effective multicelled organisms could be produced and survive. The same designer went on to create the human race with a new and higher purpose in mind. Not only would the cells within an individual cooperate with one another, but the individuals within the race would now move*

on to a new level of community responsibility, to a new kind of relationship with one another and with God.

As in the body, so in this new kind of relationship the key to success lies in the sensation of pain. All of us rejoice at the harmonious working of the human body. Yet we can but sorrow at the relationships between men. In human society we are suffering because we do not suffer enough.

So much of the sorrow in the world is due to the selfishness of one living organism that simply doesn't care when the next one suffers. In the body if one cell or group of cells grows and flourishes at the expense of the rest, we call it cancer and know that if it is allowed to spread the body is doomed. And yet, the only alternative to the cancer is absolute loyalty of every cell in the body, the head. God is calling us today to learn from the lower creation and move on to a higher level of evolution and to participate in this community which He is preparing for the salvation of the world. [1]

Cries and Whispers

Nothing unites our bodies like the pain system. An infected toenail announces to me that the toe is important, it is mine, it needs attention. If you step on my toe, I may yell "That's me!" I know it's me, because your foot is at that moment resting on a pain sensor. I am defined by pain.

When we ignore cries of pain, or perhaps grow callous and numb and let one part of our body decay unnoticed,

the body destroys itself. Remember the baby who trag-
ically chewed off her own finger because she had lost
sensation? She had no awareness that the finger was
part of her body, a part she needed to protect.

Wolves have been known to devour one of their own
hind legs when it grows numb in the winter cold. The
numbness has interrupted the unity of the body; evidently they no longer perceive the leg as being a part
of them.

Lebanon, Rhodesia, Ireland—these are loud screams
of pain from the body of Christ. The Missouri Synod rift.
The scandals of some Christian leaders. Third World
poverty. Do we listen to them, hear them, respond? Or
do we, through numbness, allow them to self-destruct,
sacrificing a limb of the body of Christ? The screams
of pain are not always so far away: there are some in
every church and office. The unemployed, divorced,
widowed, bedridden, aged ... are we listening to them?

The Christian church, by all accounts, has done a
mediocre job of acting as Christ's body through the
ages. Sometimes it has seemed to devour itself (the
Inquisition, religious wars). Yet Christ, committed to
human freedom, still relies upon us to flesh out His will
in the world, empowered by the Holy Spirit.

Listen to me who understands loyalty to the body:
"Who makes a mistake and I do not feel his sadness?
Who falls without my longing to help him? Who is spiritually hurt without my fury rising against the one who
hurt him?" (2 Cor. 11:29 LB). Or again: "Think too of all
who suffer as if you shared their pain" (Heb. 13:3 PHIL-
LIPS).

Or yet another voice:

*The church is catholic, universal, so are all her
actions; all that she does belongs to all. When
she baptizes a child, that action concerns me;
for that child is thereby connected to that body
which is my head too, and ingrafted into that
body whereof I am a member. And when she
buries a man, that action concerns me: all mankind is of one author, and is one volume; when
one man dies, one chapter is not torn out of the
book, but translated into a better language; and
every chapter must be so translated.*

*God employs several translators; some pieces
are translated by age, some by sickness, some
by war, some by justice; but God's hand is in
every translation, and His hand shall bind up
all our scattered leaves again for that library
where every book shall lie open to one another. . . .*

*No man is an island, entire of itself; every
man is a piece of the continent, a part of the
main. If a clod be washed away by the sea,
Europe is the less, as well as if a promontory
were, as well as if a manor of thy friend's or of
thine own were; any man's death diminishes
me, because I am involved in mankind, and
therefore can never send to know for whom the
bell tolls; it tolls for thee.*

*If a man carry treasure in bullion, or in a
wedge of gold, and have none coined into current money, his treasure will not defray him as
he travels. Tribulation is treasure in the nature
of it, but it is not current money in the use of
it, except we get nearer and nearer our home,*

*heaven, by it. Another may be sick too, and sick
to death, and this affliction may lie in his bowels,
as gold in a mine, and be of no use to him: but
this bell, that tells me of his affliction, digs out
and applies that gold to me: if by this consid-
eration of another's danger I take mine own into
contemplation, and so secure myself by making
my recourse to my God, who is our only secu-
rity.*[2]

Bear one another's burdens, the Bible says. It is a
lesson about pain that we all can agree to. Some of us
will not see pain as a gift; some will always accuse God
of being unfair for allowing it. But, the fact is, pain and
suffering are here among us, and we need to respond.
The response Jesus showed was to bear the burdens of
those He touched. To live in the world as His body, His
emotional incarnation, we must follow His example.

"What a wonderful God we have," Paul says. "He ...
wonderfully comforts and strengthens us in our hard-
ships and trials. And why does he do this? So that when
others are troubled, needing our sympathy and encouragement, we can pass on to them this same help
and comfort God has given us. You can be sure that
the more we undergo sufferings for Christ, the more he
will shower us with his comfort and encouragement"
(2 Cor. 1:3–5 LB).

This plan of the body meshes with the way God is
working in the world. Sometimes He does enter in, occasionally performing miracles, often giving supernatural strength to those in need. But mainly He relies on
us, His agents, to do His work in the world. We announce

His message, work for justice, pray for mercy...and suffer with the sufferers. We are to comfort each other and bring healing; by doing so, we will be recognized as Christ's body and He, the head, will get the glory.

People die in the way they have lived. Death becomes the expression of everything you are, and you can bring to it only what you have brought to your life.

Michael Roemer
Producer of *Dying*

✴ 15 ✴

A Whole New World Outside

To the person who suffers, Christianity offers one last contribution, the most important contribution of all. As we have seen, the entire Bible, 3,000 years of history and culture and human drama, focuses like a magnifying glass on the bloody death at Calvary. It is the crux of history, the cornerstone. But it is not the end of the story. Jesus did not stay on the cross. After three days in a dark tomb, He was seen alive again. Alive! Could it be? His disciples couldn't believe it at first, but He came to them, letting them feel His new body.

Christ brought us the possibility of an afterlife without

pain and suffering. All our hurts, then, are temporary. Our future will be painless. Today, we are almost embarrassed to talk about belief in an afterlife complete with rewards and punishments based on our performance on earth. An afterlife seems quaint, cowardly, "a cheap way out" of this world's problems.

Black Muslims have a funeral custom which rivals some of the Christian funeral customs in its strangeness. When the body is laid out, close friends and family encircle the casket and stand quietly, looking at the dead person. There are no tears, no flowers, no singing. Muslim sisters pass small trays from which everyone takes a thin, round patty of peppermint candy. At a given signal, the onlookers pop the candies in their mouths. Slowly the candies melt, and as they taste the sweetness, they reflect on the sweetness of the life they are commemorating. When the candy is gone . . . that, too, has meaning, for it symbolizes the end of life. It simply dissolves; there is no more.

Something in man cries out against such a belief. Where do words like "immortal" come from? Why is it murder to kill a man and not a cat?

How can it be noble to agree with the Black Muslims, the materialists, and the Marxists that this world, cancerous with evil and suffering, is the designed end for man? Such a notion only appeared after 7,000 years of recorded history. Every known primitive society and every ancient culture included elaborate beliefs in an afterlife. (Without such beliefs, archaeologists would have a much more difficult task, for the ancients conveniently buried cultural clues in tombs.)

The Coming Change

In contrast, Christians expectantly await a world where every tear will be wiped away and suffering will disappear. We have unusual metaphors to picture the afterlife—streets of gold and gates of pearl, which to the writers symbolized the paragon of luxury. Whatever heaven is, it will banish much of the discomfort of this life and usher in new, unimagined pleasures. We have shadows of it now, fleeting longings that some profound joy, which escapes so quickly here, will one day fill us.

It is as if we are locked in a dark room, as in Sartre's *No Exit*. But chinks of light are seeping through—virtue, glory, hints of truth and justice—convincing us that beyond the walls there exists a world worth all enduring.

The hope which this belief can give to a dying person is starkly illustrated in a 1976 documentary film which was shown on the Public Broadcasting System. Producer-Director Michael Roemer filmed *Dying* in Boston. The film follows the last months' activities of several terminally ill cancer patients. Two, especially, show the extremes of despair and hope.

Harriet and Bill, 33, struggle with a failure of nerve. Nervous about her own future as a widow with two sons, Harriet lashes out at her dying husband. "The longer this is dragged out, the worse this is going to be for all of us," she tells him.

"What happened to the sweet girl I married?" Bill asks. Harriet tells the interviewer: "The sweet girl is being tortured by his cancer. Who's gonna want a widow and 8- and 10-year-old sons? I don't wish him dead, but if he's gotta go why doesn't he go now?"

In the last weeks of their life together, this family

cannot cope with their fears about death. They attack each other, whining and shouting, shattering love and trust. The specter of death is too great.

Rev. Bryant, 56, the dying pastor of a black Baptist church, provides an amazing contrast. "Right now I'm living some of my greatest moments," he says. "I don't think Rockefeller could be as happy as I am."

The camera crew follows Rev. Bryant as he preaches on death to his congregation, reads the Bible to his grandchildren, and takes a trip South to visit his birthplace. He displays calm serenity and a confidence that he is merely heading home, to a place without pain.

At his funeral, the Baptist choir sings "He's Asleep." And as mourners file past the bier, some reach down to grasp his hand or pat his chest. They are losing a beloved friend, but only for a while. Rev. Bryant is facing a beginning, not an end.

Any discussion of pain is incomplete without this perspective of its temporary nature. A skilled polemist could possibly convince someone that pain is a good thing—better than any of the alternatives God could have allowed. Perhaps. But, actually, pain and suffering are far less than half the picture.

How to imagine eternity? It's so much larger than our short life here that it's hard even to visualize. You can go to a ten-foot blackboard and draw a line from one side to another. Then, make a one-inch dot in that line. To a microscopic germ cell, sitting in the midst of that one-inch dot, it would look enormous. The cell could spend its lifetime exploring its length and breadth. But you're not a germ cell, you're a human, and by stepping back to view the whole blackboard you're suddenly struck with how *huge* that ten-foot line is compared to the tiny dot that germ cell calls home.

It's the same way with eternity compared to this life. Seventy years is a long time, and we can develop a lot of ideas about God and how indifferent He appears to suffering in seventy years. But is it reasonable to judge God and His plan for the universe by the swatch of time we spend on earth? No more reasonable than for that germ cell to judge a whole blackboard by the tiny smudge of chalk where he spends his life. Is that a just trial? Have we missed the perspective of the universe and of timelessness?

Would we complain if God allowed one hour of suffering in an entire lifetime of comfort? He has allowed a lifetime which includes suffering, but that lifetime is a mere hour of eternity.

In the Christian scheme of things, this world and the time spent here are not all there is. Earth is a proving ground, a dot in eternity—but a very important dot, for Jesus said our destiny depends on our obedience here. Next time you want to cry out to God in anguished despair, blaming Him for a miserable world, remember: less than one-millionth of the evidence has been presented, and that one-millionth is being worked out under a rebel flag.

_____ **Not Yet** _____

Author Thomas Howard[1] comments that the real pain of suffering is not the present hurt—for martyrs have proved that can be endured. The real pain is that God seems to have His eyes shut, His ears stopped with wax. We read of healings in the Bible, we see others on TV ... and yet our relatives' bodies, and our own, swell with disease. Where is God? Why is He avoiding us? Why won't He answer?

The response we get is dead silence. Nothing.

The Bible is little help, for along with the healing of the widow of Nain's son are other sons who died. Peter was set loose from prison; John the Baptist was executed. Paul was used to heal people, but his own request for healing was denied.

Howard points to two surprising passages for perspective: the burial of Lazarus and the roadside talk about Jesus' death on the way to Emmaus. Immediately we object, "Yes, but both those stories have happy endings. Too few on earth have such dramatic conclusions." But we can learn from the waiting period in each story: the four days when Lazarus' body rotted in the grave and his family cried tears of disappointment over Jesus' seeming callousness, and the days when the disciples were convinced the entire kingdom had collapsed. Those four days parallel the times of anxious waiting we spend facing pain.

These crushed followers had seen Jesus heal people. Why didn't He act now? Was it that they had too little faith? How, then, to drum up more? In those middle days of gloom, it surely seemed God had deliberately passed them by.

Now, looking back at those stories, we can see how the pieces fit together. In four days, both stories received triumphant endings. Lazarus and Jesus both returned to life. Everyone rejoiced. They actually make better stories because the deaths occurred.

Howard writes of those few days of gloom:

*The point is for X-number of days their expe-
rience was of defeat. For us, alas, the "X-number of days" may be greatly multiplied. And it
is small comfort to us to be told that the difference, then, between us and, say, Mary and Martha's experience of Lazarus' death, or of the two
on the road to Emmaus, is only a quantitative
difference. "They had to wait four days. You
have to wait one, or five, or seventy years.
What's the real difference?" That is like telling
someone on the rack that his pain is only quan-
titatively different from mine with my hangnail.
The quantity is the difference. But there is, perhaps, at least this much of help for us whose
experience is that of Mary and Martha and the
others: the experience of the faithful has, in fact,
included the experience of utter death. That
seems to be part of the pattern, and it would be
hard indeed to insist that the death was attrib-
utable to some failure of faith on somebody's
part.*[2]

For all of us, not just Mary and Martha and the two
on the road to Emmaus, there will be a personal solution
of triumph. There is no slippage with God. He knows
when every sparrow falls and has every hair numbered.
Every prayer has been heard, even those which might
have seemed vacant and useless.

George MacDonald says, "The Lord has come to w'
away our tears. He is doing it; He will have it do
soon as He can; and until He can, He would hav
flow without bitterness; to which end He tells

is a blessed thing to mourn, because of the comfort on its way. Accept His comfort now, and so prepare for the comfort at hand."[3]

To view the role of pain and suffering properly, one must await the whole story. Promises of it abound in the Bible:

"And the God of all grace, who called you to his eternal glory in Christ, after you have suffered a little while, will himself restore you and make you strong, firm and steadfast" (1 Peter 5:10 NIV). "These troubles and sufferings of ours are, after all, quite small and won't last very long. Yet this short time of distress will result in God's richest blessing upon us forever and ever! So we do not look at what we can see right now, the troubles all around us, but we look forward to the joys in heaven which we have not yet seen. The troubles will soon be over, but the joys to come will last forever" (2 Cor. 4:17,18 LB).

Peter and Paul were so confident of the end result that they staked their ministries, their health, their very lives on Christ's promises.

Death and Birth

Ironically, the one event which probably causes more emotional suffering than any other—death—is in reality a translation, a time for great joy when Christ's victory will be appropriated to each of us. Describing the effect of His own death, Jesus used the simile of a woman in labor, travailing until the moment of childbirth when all is replaced by ecstasy (John 16:21).

Each of our individual deaths can be seen as a birth. Imagine what it would be like if you had had full consciousness as a fetus and could now remember those sensations:

Your world is dark, safe, secure. You are bathed in warm liquid, cushioned from shock. You do nothing for yourself; you are fed automatically, and a murmuring heartbeat assures you that someone larger than you fills all your needs. Your life consists of simple waiting—you're not sure what to wait for, but any change seems far away and scary. You meet no sharp objects, no pain, no threatening adventures. A fine existence.

One day you feel a tug. The walls are falling in on you. Those soft cushions are now pulsing and beating against you, crushing you downwards. Your body is bent double, your limbs twisted and wrenched. You're falling, upside down. For the first time in your life, you feel pain. You're in a sea of roiling matter. There is more pressure, almost too intense to bear. Your head is squeezed flat, and you are pushed harder, harder into a dark tunnel. Oh, the pain. Noise. More pressure.

You hurt all over. You hear a groaning sound and an awful, sudden fear rushes in on you. It is happening—your world is collapsing. You're sure it's the end. You see a piercing, blinding light. Cold, rough hands pull at you. A painful slap. Waaaahhhhh!

Congratulations, you have just been born.

Death is like that. On this end of the birth canal, it seems fiercesome, portentous, and full of pain. Death is a scary tunnel and we are being sucked toward it by a powerful force. None of us looks forward to it. We're afraid. It's full of pressure, pain, darkness...the unknown. But beyond the darkness and the pain there's a whole new world outside. When we wake up after death in that bright new world, our tears and hurts will be mere memories.[4] And though the new world is so much better than this one, we have no categories to really understand what it will be like. The best the Bible writers can tell us is that then, instead of the silence of God, we will have the presence of God and see Him face to face. At that time we will be given a stone, and upon it will be written a new name, which no one else knows. Our birth into new creatures will be complete (Rev. 2:17).

Do you sometimes think God does not hear? That your cries of pain fade into nothing? God is not deaf. He is as grieved by the world's trauma as you are. His only Son died here. But He has promised to set things right. Nothing simply disappears.

Let history finish. Let the symphony scratch out its last mournful note of discord before it bursts into song. As Paul said, "In my opinion whatever we may have to go through now is less than nothing compared with the magnificent future God has planned for us. The whole creation is on tiptoe to see the wonderful sight of the sons of God coming into their own....

"It is plain to anyone with eyes to see that at the present time all created life groans in a sort of universal travail. And it is plain, too, that we who have a foretaste of the Spirit are in a state of painful tension, while we wait for that redemption of our bodies which will mean that at last we have realized our full sonship in him" (Rom. 8:18,19,22,23 PHILLIPS).

As we look back on the speck of eternity that was the history of this planet, we will be impressed not by its importance, but by its diminutiveness. From the viewpoint of the Andromeda galaxy, the holocaustic destruction of our entire solar system would be barely visible, a match flaring faintly in the distance, then imploding in permanent darkness. Yet for this burnt-out match, God sacrificed Himself.

Pain can be seen, as Berkouwer puts it, as the great "not yet" of eternity. It reminds us of where we are, and fans in us a thirst for where we will someday be.

At the height of his suffering, Job spoke:

> *How I wish someone would record what I am*
> * saying*
> *Or with a chisel carve my words in stone,*
> *and write them so they would last forever.*
> *But I know there is someone in heaven*
> *who will come at last to my defense.*
> *I will see him with my own eyes,*
> *and he will not be a stranger.*
>   *(Job 19:23ff. Job for Modern Man)*

I can believe that one day every bruise and every leukemia cell and every embarrassment and every hurt will be set right, and all those grim moments of hoping against hope will be rewarded.

_____ **Where Is God When It Hurts?** _____

For a good portion of my life, I shared the viewpoint of those who rail against God for allowing pain. Suffering pressed in too close. I could find no way to rationalize a world as malignant as this one.

As I visited those whose pain far exceeded my own, though, I was surprised by its effects. Suffering was as likely to produce strengthened faith as to sow agnosticism. And as I visited those with Hansen's disease, particularly, I was convinced of the important role of pain in the world.

In one sense, there will be no solution to pain until Jesus returns and recreates the earth. I am sustained by faith in that great hope. If I did not truly believe that God is a Physician and not a Sadist, and that He "feels in Himself the tortured presence of every nerve that lacks its response," I would immediately abandon all attempts to plumb the mysteries of suffering. My anger about pain has melted mostly for one reason: I have come to know God. He has given me joy and love and happiness and goodness. They have come in flashes, in the midst of my confused, unrighteous world, but their presence has been absolute enough to convince me that my God is worthy of trust. Knowing Him is worth all enduring.

Where does that leave me when I stand next to a hospital bed the next time a close friend gets Hodgkin's disease? After all, this search started at a bedside. It leaves me with a solid faith in a Person which no amount of suffering can erode. And, because Christianity is worked out in a real world among real people, I also need a few reassurances to grasp the role of suffering in the world.

Where is God when it hurts?

He has been there from the beginning, designing a pain system that still, in the midst of a fallen, rebellious world, bears the stamp of His genius and equips us for life on this planet.

He has watched us reflect His image, carving out great works of art, launching mighty adventures, living out this earth in a mixture of pain and pleasure when the two so closely coalesce they sometimes become almost indistinguishable.

He has used pain, even in its grossest forms, to teach us, asking us to let it turn us to Him. He has stooped to conquer.

He has watched this rebellious planet live on, mercifully allowing the human project to continue its self-guided way.

He has let us cry out and echo Job with louder and harsher fits of anger against Him, blaming Him for a world we spoiled.

He has allied Himself with the poor and suffering, establishing a kingdom tilted in their favor, which the rich and powerful often shun.

He has promised supernatural strength to nourish our spirit, even if our physical suffering goes unrelieved.

He has joined us. He has hurt and bled and cried and suffered. He has dignified for all time those who suffer by sharing their pain.

He is with us now, ministering to us through His Spirit and through members of His body who are commissioned to bear us up and relieve our suffering for the sake of the head.

He is waiting, gathering the armies of good. One day He will unleash them. The world will see one last explosion of pain before the full victory is ushered in. Then, He will create for us a new, incredible world. And pain shall be no more.

> *Listen, I tell you a mystery: We shall not all sleep, but we shall all be changed—in a flash, in the twinkling of an eye, at the last trumpet. For the trumpet will sound, the dead will be*

*raised imperishable, and we shall be changed.
For the perishable must clothe itself with the
imperishable, and the mortal with immortality.
When the perishable has been clothed with the
imperishable, and the mortal with immortality,
then the saying that is written will come true:
"Death has been swallowed up in victory."*

"Where, O death, is your victory?

*Where, O death is your sting?" (1 Cor.
15:51–55 NIV).*

Sources

CHAPTER 1

[1]C. E. M. Joad, *God and Evil* (New York: Harper and Brothers Publishers, 1943), p. 28.

CHAPTER 2

[1]R. J. Christman, *Sensory Experience* (Scranton, Pa.: Intext Educational Publishers, 1971), p. 359.

[2]Ibid., p. 361.

[3]Maurice Burton, *The Sixth Sense of Animals* (New York: Taplinger Publishing Company, 1972), p. 9.

CHAPTER 4

[1]Christman, *Sensory Experience*, p. 359.

CHAPTER 5

[1]G.K. Chesterton, *Orthodoxy* (Garden City, N.Y.: Doubleday and Company, Inc., 1959), p. 144.

[2]Jay Kesler and Tim Stafford, *I Never Promised You a Disneyland* (Waco, Tex.: Word Books, Inc., 1975), p. 85.

[3]Chesterton, *Orthodoxy*, p. 78.

[4]Ibid., p. 80.

CHAPTER 6

[1]"A Luckless City Buries Its Dead," *Time*, June 7, 1976.

[2]John W. Wenham, *The Goodness of God* (Downers Grove, Ill.: InterVarsity Press, 1974), p. 73.

[3]Albert Camus, *The Plague* (New York: Vintage Books, 1972), p. 203.

[4]"In Tornados, Some Trust God," *Psychology Today*, August 1974, p. 36.

[5]Leslie D. Weatherhead, *Why Do Men Suffer?* (London: Student Christian Movement Press, Inc., 1935).

[6]John Hick, *Philosophy of Religion* (Englewood Cliffs, N.J.: Prentice-Hall, Inc., 1963), chap. 3.

[7]C. S. Lewis, *The Problem of Pain* (New York: The Macmillan Company, 1962), pp. 39,40,42.

CHAPTER 7

[1]Elie Wiesel, *Night* (New York: Avon Books, 1969), p. 9.
[2]Ibid.
[3]Ibid, pp. 8–9.
[4]Ibid, p. 10.

CHAPTER 8

[1]Brian Sternberg with John Poppy, "My Search for Faith," *Look*, March 10, 1964, pp. 79–80.
[2]Ibid.

CHAPTER 10

[1]Lewis, *The Problem of Pain*, p. 108.
[2]Richard Batey, *Jesus and the Poor* (New York: Harper & Row, Publishers, 1972), p. 19.
[3]George MacDonald, *Life Essential* (Wheaton, Ill.: Harold Shaw Publishers, 1974), pp. 43–44.
[4]Paraphrase from John Donne, *Devotions* (Ann Arbor, Mich.: University of Michigan Press, 1959), pp. 15–16.

CHAPTER 11

[1]James D. Hardy and Harold G. Wolff and Helen Goodell, *Pain Sensations and Reactions* (New York: Haffner Publishing Co., 1967), pp. 299–301.
[2]Mark Krum, "The Face of Pain," *Sports Illustrated*, March 8, 1976, p. 60.
[3]Ibid, p. 62.
[4]Donne, *Devotions*, p. 36
[5]Douglas Colligan, "That Helpless Feeling: The Dangers of Stress," *New York*, July 14, 1975, p. 28.
[6]Ibid., p. 32.
[7]Ibid., p. 31.
[8]Ibid., p. 30.
[9]Ibid.
[10]Hardy, *Pain Sensations and Reactions*, p. 117.

CHAPTER 12

[1]George Mangakis, "Letter in a Bottle," *Atlantic Monthly*, October 1971, p. 253.

CHAPTER 13

[1]Robert Coles, *Children of Crisis, Vol. 2: Migrants, Mountaineers, and Sharecroppers* (Philadelphia: Atlantic Monthly Press, 1967–1971).

[2]Dorothy L. Sayers, *Christian Letters to a Post-Christian World* (Grand Rapids, Mich.: William B. Eerdmans Publishing Company, 1969), p. 14.

[3]T. S. Eliot, *Collected Poems 1904–1962* (New York: Harcourt, Brace & World, Inc.), p. 187.

CHAPTER 14

[1]Dorothy Clark Wilson, *Ten Fingers for God* (New York: McGraw-Hill Book Co., 1965), pp. 145ff.

[2]Donne, *Devotions*, pp. 107–109.

CHAPTER 15

[1]Thomas Howard, "On Brazen Heavens," *Christianity Today*, December 7, 1973, pp. 8–11.

[2]Ibid., pp. 9–10.

[3]MacDonald, *Life Essential*, p. 54.

[4]Joseph Bayly was the essential source for this analogy.

Winner of the Gold Medallion Award for the Best Inspirational Book of 1977, *Where is God When it Hurts?* deals realistically with crisis, pain, and suffering. Philip Yancey has entered the world of the sufferer to find out what difference it makes to be a Christian there.